The Legacy Code Programmer's Toolbox

Practical skills for software professionals working with legacy code

Jonathan Boccara

The Legacy Code Programmer's Toolbox

Practical skills for software professionals working with legacy code

Jonathan Boccara

This is a Leanpub book. Leanpub empowers authors and publishers with the Lean Publishing process. Lean Publishing is the act of publishing an in-progress ebook using lightweight tools and many iterations to get reader feedback, pivot until you have the right book and build traction once you do.

© 2018 - 2019 Jonathan Boccara

To Elisabeth

Contents

Foreword 1
Acknowledgments 5
Introduction: There is a lot of legacy, out there . 9
    Legacy code 9
    You didn't become a developer for this 11
    There is a lot of legacy, out there 13

Part I: Approaching legacy code 17

Chapter 1: The right attitude to deal with legacy code 19
    The natural reaction: who the f*** wrote this . . 20
    A humble view of legacy code 21
    The efficient approach: taking ownership 25
    Having a role model 27

CONTENTS

Chapter 2: How to use bad code to learn how to write great code 31
    Don't like the code? Elaborate, please. 32
    The vaccine against bad code is bad code 36
    Be aware of what good code looks like 39

Chapter 3: Why reading good code is important (and where to find it) 43
    The importance of reading good code 44
    Where to find good code 46
    Become more efficient with legacy code 53

Part II: 10 techniques to understand legacy code 55

Chapter 4: 3 techniques to get an overview of the code 57
    1) Choosing a stronghold 58
    2) Starting from the inputs and outputs of the program (and how to find them) 63
    3) Analysing well-chosen stacks 65

Chapter 5: 4 techniques to become a code speed-reader 73
    1) Working your way backwards from the function's outputs 75
    2) Identifying the terms that occur frequently . 79
    3) Filtering on control flow 101
    4) Distinguishing the main action of the function 109

Chapter 6: 3 techniques to understand code in detail 123
    1) Using "practice" functions to improve your code-reading skills 124
    2) Decoupling the code. 125
    3) Teaming up with other people 134
    It gets easier with practice 136

Part III: Knowledge 139

Chapter 7: Knowledge is Power 141
    Where did the knowledge go? 142

Chapter 8: How to make knowledge flow in your team 149
    Writing precious documentation 150
    Telling your tales: acquiring knowledge in Eager mode 158
    Knowing who to ask: getting knowledge in Lazy mode 159
    Pair-programming and mob-programming . . . 160
    External sources of knowledge 162
    Make the knowledge flow 163

Chapter 9: The Dailies: knowledge injected in regular doses 165
    What are Dailies? 166
    Monthly sessions 168
    The major benefits of Dailies 170
    There is plenty of content out there 171

CONTENTS

Be the one who spreads knowledge 173

Part IV: Cutting through legacy code 175

Chapter 10: How to find the source of a bug without knowing a lot of code 177
The slowest way to find the source of a bug . . . 178
The quickest way to find the source of a bug . . 179
A binary search for the root cause of a bug . . . 182
A case study 184

Chapter 11: The Harmonica School: A case study in diagnosing a bug quickly in an unfamiliar code base 187
Lesson subscriptions 189
Let's find the source of that bug, quickly 192
The more time you spend in the application, the less total time you spend debugging . . . 208

Chapter 12: What to fix and what *not* to fix in a legacy codebase 211
Legacy code is a bully 212
The value-based approach (a.k.a. "Hit it where it hurts") 214
Where does it hurt? 223
Use the value-based approach 228

Chapter 13: 5 refactoring techniques to make long functions shorter **231**
   The birth of a Behemoth 232
   Identifying units of behaviour 233
   1) Extract `for` loops 235
   2) Extract intensive uses of the same object ... 238
   3) Raise the level of abstraction in unbalanced
      `if` statements 244
   4) Lump up pieces of data that stick together .. 249
   5) Follow the hints in the layout of the code .. 253
   6) Bonus: using your IDE to hide code 255
   The impact on performance 258

Conclusion: The legacy of tomorrow **261**
   The bigger picture of writing code 262
   How to deal with legacy code 263
   But you're also person A 264
   Parting words 264

References **267**

Foreword

What we have built is in the past. Where we are is the present. Where we want to be is the future.

Welcome to code. Welcome to the human condition. Welcome to the joys and frustrations of code, to the complexities of the human condition and to what happens when they meet and find themselves drawn into an intimate long-term relationship. Legacy code is as much about the people who surround and work in the code as it is about the code itself.

The default developer response to legacy code is primal. The fight-or-flight response kicks in, logic gives way to emotion, the question "What does the code need?" is replaced by "How can I spend as little time in this code as possible?" This is the thinking of short-term survival, not of long-term living, the habit of defend and attack, not of peace and construction.

To calm our response, we need first to appreciate that legacy code was not created arbitrarily or maliciously. Inasmuch as it may have been written in ignorance, this is because we are always operating with incomplete knowledge – and yes, that *we* includes you right now.

No matter what we may think of it, code is created systematically. Perhaps not always with a system of thinking and practice that is deliberate or appreciated, but we should understand that it is not arbitrary. The code was written by people – in which we must include our past selves – who were responding to a situation with the tools – and the emotions and the knowledge and... – that they had available to them at the time. Start from there. There are no winners in a blame game.

To understand the system of code we should acknowledge the system of people and practices that created it, we should journey to retrieve the meaning in the legacy and make ways forward possible. There is an underappreciated ingenuity here, an application of time and tools and humanity that deserves our attention. This is what Jonathan is offering you in this book.

But rather than keep legacy at arms length, Jonathan brings it close. Legacy is very real and no one legacy is exactly like another, so you need a toolbox, not a silver bullet. And he understands and wants to help you. This is a book of compassion and intelligence.

If development in legacy code is a journey, Jonathan is your patient and loyal companion. He has stories for the road, ideas to help you on your way and suggestions for the route. He's also brought his tools along and invited you to share.

It is easy to forget that outside the world of software development, the word *legacy* has another meaning. A positive meaning, a gift of wealth from the past to the present for the future. This book will help you reclaim the word.

Kevlin Henney

Acknowledgments

Writing a book is quite some work, and not something one does alone. Several people have helped me shape this book, sometimes influencing it profoundly. And I suspect some of them aren't completely aware of the impact they had on it.

Now is my chance to express my gratitude.

My first thanks go to my dear wife, Elisabeth. Your invariable support has given me the means to stay motivated in the project of writing what I know about legacy code. I'm very grateful for your patience, for the interest you took in the project of this book as well as your kind understanding for the time it demanded. Your wise advice, that makes the most intricate matters look simple, was of an invaluable help. From all my heart, thank you.

I thank Patrice Dalesme who was my manager for many years. Patrice picked me up in his team as a young sprout who knew next to nothing, and undertook to teach me professional programming. On the top of caring about writing good code, Patrice has taught me how to create value and have a fulfilling professional life while working with existing code, either explicitly or simply be having him as a role model (some call him "King Patrice" or even "Magic Patrice"). Without him, I wouldn't have had much to say in this book. Few people have the chance to work with a developer and manager like you. You rock.

When I was considering taking on the enterprise of writing *The Legacy Code Programmer's Toolbox*, I started by crafting an introduction along with the list of topics I intended to address. I showed it to several people, in order to test it and decide for a go or no-go for the project. Their warm enthusiasm for this project made it a full-speed go, and I'm grateful they encouraged me to carry on. These people are Ben Deane, Bryan St. Amour, Clare Macrae, Eric Pederson, Frédéric Tingaud, Ivan Čukić, Kate Gregory, Marco Arena, Philippe Bourgau and Ólafur Waage.

I also want to thank Kevlin Henney for his inspiration, feedback and support, and for writing the foreword of this book.

And last but not least, my gratitude goes to all the people who reviewed the book, that spent time and sweat in its construction along with me. The feedback that each of you gave has transformed the book in its way, and this makes you part of it. A big thank you to Arne Mertz, Avi Lachmish, Bartłomiej Filipek, Barney Dellar, Bilel Belhadj, Clare Macrae, Eric Roussel, Feng Lee, Francisco Castillo, Ivan Čukić, Javier Sogo, Jean-François Lots, JFT, Kobi, Kyle Shores, Marc-Anton Böhm, Matthieu Poullet, Miguel Raggi, Nikolai Wuttke, Rakesh UV, Riccardo Brugo, Swarup Sahoo, Thomas Benard, and Yves Dolce.

Finally, amongst the reviewers, I want to dedicate a special thanks to Phillip Johnston, Ricardo Nabinger Sanchez and

Tim van Deurzen, for the impressive amount of work in their reviews and the meticulous analyses they performed to produce them.

Introduction: There is a lot of legacy, out there

Hello, brave sailor in the ocean of legacy!

If you're opening this book, I'm assuming that you have to deal with legacy code on a regular basis, if not every day, in your job as a software developer. And I am also assuming that you are resolved to face it, learn from it, thrive in it, and live on a happy life.

If those assumptions are correct, then you've come to the right place. This book will give you insights on how to perceive legacy code, how to act on it, how to act on your fellow developers, and how to live a happy life (well, to the extent that legacy code is concerned, that is!).

Legacy code

First things first. Let's start by agreeing on what we call legacy code. You have a fair idea of what that is, I do too, but let's make sure that we're in line.

Introduction: There is a lot of legacy, out there

There are several definitions of legacy code out there. For example, in his book *Working Effectively with Legacy Code*, Michael Feathers defines legacy code as code without tests.

Wikipedia gives a more formal definition, that is "source code that relates to a no-longer supported or manufactured operating system or other computer technology."

There are also less formal definitions, for example some people call legacy code the code that was written before they arrived in a company.

For our purpose, we will use a definition that tries to stick to the meaning of legacy code in usage, the one you probably thought about when reading this book's cover.

When we talk about legacy code, we will mean code that:

1. is hard for you to understand,
2. you're not comfortable changing,
3. and you're somehow concerned with.

Note that under this definition, someone's legacy code can be someone else's normal code. Indeed, according to part **1)**, a piece of code can be hard to understand for you, but easier for another person (the person who wrote it, for instance).

In practice, there can be spots in a codebase that constitute legacy code for pretty much every developer of the team.

Also note that part **2)** of the definition ties up with the "code without tests" definition. If there are no tests around a piece of code, you won't be comfortable changing it. Our definition is not quite the same as Michael Feathers's though, because even if a piece of code has *some* tests around it, it doesn't necessarily mean that you're comfortable changing it; for instance if only few cases are covered.

Finally, for it to be legacy for you, a piece of code must concern you. There is plenty of code on the planet that you'd have trouble to understand and would feel quite uncomfortable changing. And it's not legacy code for you. It's code that you don't care about. Hence part **3)** in the definition.

You didn't become a developer for this

Legacy code can be hard to take on, especially at the beginning of your career, when you come in on your first day, excited to be paid for spending your days programming.

Indeed, legacy code looks nothing like what schools teach. If you studied computer science, you typically got assigned to projects that you built from the ground up.

You understood them well because you designed sizeable parts, if not all, of their structure. You felt comfortable changing them for the same reason, and in fact you didn't have to change them so much, because you weren't maintaining them for years.

If you're a self-taught programmer, you had total freedom to choose what to work with, and you were driven by your interest. You could start an exciting project, interrupt it to build a library for it, interrupt it to build another library to implement a cool pattern you had just learned, and so on.

Programming small projects is extremely rewarding. You can see your program grow very quickly, you add features almost as fast as you think of them, and very rarely encounter the concept of "regression". Joy.

And one day you get into professional programming. While you still get to interact a lot with code, things work differently. There is existing code, to begin with. And to add features you need to figure out how this existing code works.

Then you need to be very cautious when you add a feature, because it could have an impact on this existing code. So you have to spend time writing tests, maybe even refactor existing code in order to write tests, deal with regressions, and accept that it's not so fast and easy any more.

And you face legacy code. It can be daunting. You need to understand someone else's writing, or plenty of people's writings combined. You have to think about why they did what they did. You have to understand the structures in the code and how they relate together.

All this understanding demands some intellectual effort, especially if it is legacy code (because of part **1)** of the definition), and it's much less of a smooth ride than writing your own code.

What's more, you have to modify it! As a developer, you're paid for changing code, not only for staring at it and trying to figure it out. And part **2)** of the definition of legacy code puts you in a difficult position.

Recognizing yourself in this yet? If so, then great, because this book is targeted at you.

There is a lot of legacy, out there

When you think about it, all this makes sense: you're not working on the same sort of application as when you were a young sprout learning to program.

The implementation you're making now is helping people on a day-to-day basis. It will be there for a long time hopefully, you make a living out of it, and your customers expect a level of quality and richness of features that you can't get out of a single developer. And even less out of a single developer hopping from project to project.

The first thing I want you to realize is that you and your company are **not the only ones facing legacy code**. Far from that.

I've worked with large codebases (in the tens of millions of lines of code), I'm an organizer of a Software Crafters meetup, I go to a decent number of conferences, and I run a popular blog about making code more expressive (fluentcpp.com[1]). In all those places, I get to meet people that deal with legacy code on a daily basis.

And I can tell you, legacy code is everywhere.

Some people don't realize this and feel like they're out of luck, because they ended up in a place where programming isn't as fun as it used to be for them.

The bright side for you is that if you face legacy code, it's normal. You don't have to flee your company just because of this, since the other one down the street will certainly also have legacy code.

And the even brighter side is that there is a way for you to be happy with the reality of programming. This is what this book is about.

Here is the program: we will start off with the right attitude to deal with legacy code (Chapter 1), then we'll move on to how to use legacy code to improve your programming skills (Chapter 2) and where to find good code to get some inspiration (Chapter 3). This constitutes Part I of the book, about approaching legacy code.

Part II is about understanding the code itself. It covers 10 techniques to understand code you don't know. Those techniques are spread across three chapters: how to get an overview of the code (Chapter 4), how to become a code speed-reader (Chapter 5) and how to understand code in detail (Chapter 6).

---

[1]https://www.fluentcpp.com

Then in Part III we will dive into the topic of knowledge. We will see why in legacy code Knowledge is Power (Chapter 7), how to make knowledge flow around your team (Chapter 8) and focus on a specific practice to inject regular doses of knowledge: the Dailies (Chapter 9).

In Part IV, we'll see how to cut through legacy code, by jumping to the places that matter to find the source of a bug quickly (Chapters 10 & 11), deciding when to refactor the code to add value to it or when to leave it alone (Chapter 12), and clearing out long functions by making them shorter (Chapter 13)

Hoping to change your reality of programming with legacy code, let's begin.

Part I: Approaching legacy code

Chapter 1: The right attitude to deal with legacy code
Chapter 2: How to use bad code to learn how to write great code
Chapter 3: Why reading good code is important (and where to find it)

Chapter 1: The right attitude to deal with legacy code

Over the years I've had the time to experience how it *feels* to work with legacy code, and I have watched and discussed with many developers who also expressed their feelings about it.

A lot of developers have a hard time working with legacy code. Day in and day out, they trudge through their tasks by interacting with it.

But a few people seem to breeze through their tasks, even if those imply working with legacy code. It's not that they have super powers, but they seem to not mind working with legacy code, and even display a positive attitude in the face of tasks that would rebuke others.

I believe that there are two mindsets regarding legacy code: the natural mindset, and the effective mindset.

The people who win through are those that stick to the effective mindset. On the other hand, those that stick to the natural mindset have a harder time going on with their jobs dealing with software.

Let's see what those two mindsets are about.

The natural reaction: who the f*** wrote this

Picture yourself navigating a legacy codebase.

You're looking for something, and what you stumble across is a pile of tangled code that you can't make any sense of. Or some code that looks very poorly written. Or both.

How do you react?

One of the possible reactions is the natural - or primal - one. It consists in deciding that:

- This code is a pile of crap,
- The person who wrote it had no idea what they were doing,
- You would have done such a better job,
- You're way better than this, maybe you should find another place that deserves your skills.

Have you ever felt that way? I've seen many people do so. I've experienced it myself before I knew better.

And it's normal, because that's what this mindset is: *primal*. That's what we're wired to do, for whatever psychological reason that makes us feel good about it.

A primal attitude is fantastic though, if you're fighting against a gorilla in the jungle, or if you're being pursued by a serial killer in a dark alley.

But in software development, the primal attitude sucks.

As a software developer, you're paid for being rational, not for being primal. And if you look at legacy code the rational way, quite a few things start looking different.

I don't imply that the primal feeling always leads to the wrong conclusion. Maybe a particular piece of code is crap, maybe it was written by somebody who wasn't qualified, and maybe you ought to be somewhere else.

But often, putting on your rational hat offers a brand-new perspective on a piece of code. And if you're a software developer, it is a splendid rational hat that you're wearing. So let's dress up and put it on: let's see legacy code for what it really is.

A humble view of legacy code

Legacy code is not your enemy. In fact, when you think about it, we may go as far as saying that we can be software developers *thanks* to legacy code.

Legacy code made the application grow

How is that? The early stages of development of a piece of software are the crucial moments where it took off, captured clients, built on cash, and created a brand and image to its customers. This was done with a product, and behind it was the code.

Some of this code may be still around now. Some of it may not be around, but affected the architecture in a way that has left traces until today. But it is this code that performed the features that your customers liked your company for in the first place. This is legacy code. This is your legacy, and without it you would probably not have a job today.

The amount of work put into a legacy codebase is often colossal, if you add up all the time invested by every developer that worked on it. Legacy code typically contains lots of features, and a myriad of bugfixes. If you were to start from scratch you'd have to go through most of the bug analyses again, and fix them.

Now let's try to look at a piece of legacy code for what it really is, by putting ourselves in the shoes of the person who wrote it.

Legacy code has time on its side

Legacy code is often more or less old. If you mentally travel back to the time it was written, do you think people knew as much as you do today?

Did the person who wrote it know the best practices that we are slowly putting together as a development community over the years? Did anyone know at that time?

Could they anticipate the direction that today's programming languages, Modern C++, the latest versions of Java, Python, JavaScript, and so on, were taking, and that is now so familiar to us?

Some legacy code that is around now has been written when some of us where in school (and for some in the early stages of school). Back then, technology wasn't what it is today, and conversely, a disturbing thought is that the best code we can write now might be laughed at in ten years.

So if we were in the actual position of the person who wrote that code, it may well be that we wouldn't have done such a better job.

What's even more humbling is to take the time to think about how we would have solved the problem that some code is trying to solve.

Surveying a piece of legacy code at a glance, we can see things that seem absurd, and our reptilian brain starts sending out this feeling of superiority to its friend the higher brain: "had I been given the chance, I would have done so much better".

Well, maybe we would have done better. But often, when we actually try to solve the problem, with all the technical and functional constraints surrounding it, we become aware of certain things that prevent us from doing an elegant design. Things we hadn't seen at first sight.

You never really know until you actually try it. And even then, you may not know until some tests (or in the worst case, some customers) bring up an issue coming from the design.

Seeing legacy code for *who* it really is

Still being rational, that picture of an evil and under-qualified person writing ridiculous code to make your life hard doesn't fit the reality for at least one simple reason: it's not just one person.

Legacy code becomes tangled and difficult to understand because of an inconsistent accumulation of changes, made by many people, who sometimes weren't even employed by the company at the same time.

Consider the very first version of the code. Maybe it made some sense, but didn't express its intentions well. Then the developer who took it on next may have understood it a bit differently, adding a change that wasn't exactly in line with what the code was designed for. But it still wasn't too bad. And then the next person arrived, gave yet another new direction to the code, and so on.

When you add this all up with many people over many years, what you get is a chunky piece of legacy code (this is why being expressive is such a determining characteristic of success for code).

Therefore, the code you see today that made you - primally - want to hit someone with a club over their head, doesn't have one culprit. To be really fair, you would have to go find many people, some of them off doing other projects, and gently tap each head with your club, over which you would have placed a cushion before. This way, you would spread your punishing blow out equitably. Alternatively, you could pick someone at random to bash, but there is no way that could be called fair.

Finally, let's ask ourselves a challenging question: didn't we also write legacy code? When you look back at the code you wrote a while ago, do you find it crystal clear and elegant?

First of all, there is a context that we have when we're "in the zone" when coding, that we lack when looking at code just out of the blue.

But above all, you should almost *hope* that you don't like your past code too much. Indeed, if you look at code you wrote a year ago and don't find it could be improved, it means you haven't learned much over the past year - and that is definitely not what you want.

The efficient approach: taking ownership

Now that you see legacy code with a rational eye, what can you do in practice to quit the primal mindset and join those in the efficient mindset?

The first thing to do is: **don't complain if you are not intending to improve the code.**

Complaining for the sake of it is just making noise, and a harmful one. Moaning about how you don't understand a piece of code, or how terribly designed it is, or how you don't like it in any way won't get you anywhere.

Worse, it is a self-fulfilling prophecy that won't help you handle legacy code better at all, quite the contrary. It puts you in the position of a victim, not the one of an active player.

More than just you, this affects the people around you. Someone who criticizes the code just for the sake of it sets an example, and little by little the team gets used to this. It creates an atmosphere where people see around them that it's the normal thing to just blame the code.

This is particularly contagious to the younger persons of the team. If you have young developers around you, or if you are a manager of younger developers, choose to be a model for them in terms of attitude. It's a bit like watching your language around kids so that they don't get a bad vocabulary.

And if you do have people that make non-constructive complaints around you, make an active effort to not get sucked in. Don't criticize the code just for the sake of it. Be particularly careful to this if you're towards the beginning of your career, so that you grow positive habits.

The second aspect of the efficient mindset is to **consider that the code you're working on is *your* code.**

Whether you wrote it yourself or not, however good or bad you think it is, this is your code and you have responsibility over it.

Note that taking ownership is not the same as taking the blame - for whatever bad design somebody had to come up with before you even graduated. It means acknowledging that you are the one in charge now. Indeed, even if you're not a manager, you are in charge of at least some portion of the code.

Entering this mindset transforms the way you see legacy code. It's no longer something that some people, distant in time and space, have written and that you can criticize at will to show how bad it is and how good we are. It is your code, and you are here to make the most out of it.

When I came across this mindset (thanks to my fantastic manager Patrice Dalesme) I became motivated to do whatever was in my power to understand my code, improve it, and create business value out of it. Several years later, I'm still just as motivated to do so.

Having a role model

Having a model helps a lot to settle into the right mindset. Try to identify a developer from your company that is in the effective mindset, and get inspired by them, as with a mentor. It's practical if it is your manager, but it doesn't have to be. That person may even not know that you're taking inspiration from them.

How to identify which developers are in the right mindset around you? Look at who gives the impression not to mind tackling hard legacy pieces of code!

Even if you can't change the past and how code was written, you have the power to control your attitude, and this will affect the future of how you work. Choosing the right mindset makes a difference, be there in your efficiency as a developer or in your happiness as a person in day-to-day life.

It's always a good time to enter the efficient mindset, and the perfect moment to do this is... now. Take responsibility, take ownership.

Key takeaways

- Suspect that writing the code you're reading must have been harder than it looks.
- Realize that code difficult to read is not the work of one evil character.
- Avoid complaining if you don't intend to improve the code.
- Take ownership of the part of the codebase you're working on.
- Find a role model to get inspired by their attitude.

Chapter 2: How to use bad code to learn how to write great code

Software developers need to learn.

This is a basic, fundamental need carved into our genes, and for a lot of us this is even how we came to software development in the first place: the desire to discover new things.

The problem is, with legacy code, you don't exactly get to discover innovations so often. Or sometimes you discover things in your codebase that you'd have preferred not to know about.

When interacting with old code that you have trouble understanding, what you get to learn tends to be specific knowledge about how the codebase is organized out rather than how to get better as a software developer.

And not improving your skills is dangerous in the long term. It is detrimental for your career: as years go by, you're supposed to get better at software design. And what's more, stagnating at the same skill level can make your motivation wither and die in your everyday life.

In short, you want to keep improving your skills as a software developer.

But can someone improve their coding skills if all they have to deal with all day is legacy code of questionable quality?

The answer is Yes. Here are three techniques that will help you do so.

Don't like the code? Elaborate, please.

Think about the last time you saw a piece of code that you didn't like. It could be the implementation of a function, the contents of a class, a prototype in an interface, anything.

By the way, you may wonder if not liking a piece of code doesn't conflict with the efficient mindset we discuss in Chapter 1. I don't think it does: the bare fact of taking responsibility of the code doesn't make it better. It makes you more able to tackle it, but you still can (and should) evaluate objectively the quality of your code.

So you're facing this piece of code that you don't like. What should you do in practice? Should you move on to something else? Or should you refactor it?

Both are valid options depending on how much this code is hindering you (which is discussed in details in Chapter 12), but there is something that you can do in all cases: **explain why you don't like it**. What's wrong with that particular piece of code? If you don't like it, there must be something wrong with it, right?

If it's just a matter of style, then don't dwell on it. If an opening brace is not on the new line and you happen to prefer it to be on the new line, or the other way round, just move on. Your time is too valuable to argue on trivial issues. Here we're talking about your feeling there must be something inherently wrong with a piece of code.

More often than not, the reason why it is bad code is not so easy to pinpoint. Try it and you'll be surprised. We can judge a piece of code as "good" or "bad" in a matter of seconds, but articulating what's wrong with it takes longer. And sometimes a lot longer.

By formulating what's wrong, I mean being very, very detailed in the articulation of what makes this code bad. Don't stop at "it's too complex" or "it's unclear" or, worse, at "it makes me sick". There are a hundred reasons that can make code complex or unclear, or that can make you sick. The point is to be precise, and this is what takes an effort.

As an example, it once took me several days on and off to put my finger on what was bothering me in a certain function interface. I sensed that something was wrong with that function, however each of its part was looking all right when taken separately. Yet somehow, when put together that function interface didn't seem clear to me.

And then I realized it: it was the names of the parameters. The names of the parameters were at the level of abstraction of the calling code, which semantically bound them to it.

More precisely, that function was comparing its parameters together, and those were called something like `valueBefore` and `valueAfter`. The function did not make any assumption related to time, but its parameters were called that only because that function was used in a context with two values that happened to represent different versions of an object in time.

A different context needing that function would find the parameters names confusing, making the interface harder to use correctly. Better names would be `value1` and `value2`, to show that it could be used with any two objects to compare, and not only objects at different points in time. Once I had seen it, it was obvious it was what was making me uncomfortable.

What this technique will bring you

But what's the point of putting the time and effort to pin down what is wrong in bad code in excruciating details?

There are at least three advantages: becoming more familiar with the code, seeing how code is structured and, most importantly: **learning what to pay attention to.**

The first two advantages go together. By dissecting the code, if only mentally, you will become more familiar with it. And becoming more familiar with a region of the code, however small it is, gives you an anchor point that you can use later to uncover more code. More on this in Chapter 4 about how to get an overview of the code.

Also, the more you analyse a piece of code, the more aspects of it you're considering. This lets you touch upon the various components that make a piece of code what it is. When scrutinizing the code that was bothering you, you will at first examine certain aspects of it that turn out to be ok. And then you'll hit the spot.

Indeed at some point, when you figure out what it was exactly that was disturbing you, you will find the flaw (or flaws) of the piece of code you were analysing.

This type of flaw is something that one *can* get wrong. And knowing this has great value, because you are now aware of one more thing in code to pay attention to, in order to write good code. You can then **apply this knowledge to other pieces of code** that you design in the future. Since that story with parameter names, it's something I've been paying attention to, and it made my interfaces clearer.

The more time you spend searching in order to be accurate in your description, the more you learn when you finally discover the exact nature of the problem.

Share your findings

Once you have found an aspect of coding to pay attention to, what helps a lot is to explain it to other people. This helps because it allows you to articulate your idea clearly enough for someone who doesn't know about the code to understand it.

If worst come to worst, you can talk it out with a rubber duck, but try to share it with other people. It can be a casual talk at the coffee machine, or it can be a presentation, or a blog article (if you don't have a blog but would like to write about writing clean code, consider guest posting[2] on Fluent C++ for example)

Whichever way, you want to get this outside of your own mind to get a clearer picture about what you discovered.

The vaccine against bad code is bad code

This was the first of the three guidelines: elaborating on why you don't like a particular piece of code. The second guideline is a corollary of the first one, and it applies after having changed code to improve it, for example with a refactoring.

There is one thing we're all tempted to do after finishing a refactoring: crossing it off our to-do list, and walk away knowing we've made the world (or at least, the codebase) a better place. What's more satisfying than that?

But before you go enjoy this feeling, I urge you to do one last thing: think about **why the code is now better than before you changed it**.

---

[2] https://www.fluentcpp.com/write-for-us

Once again, it's not just about stating the code has become "simpler" or "clearer", or "doesn't make me sick any more". It's still about formulating as precisely as possible what has been improved in the piece of code.

Let me give you an example. We teamed up once with a colleague to refactor an `if` statement that combined several conditions in an intricate way. Since that `if` statement got in our way of understanding the code every time we read that portion of code, we decided to make it simpler. And before starting, we didn't know what "simpler" would look like for that `if` statement.

After struggling with the code and shuffling the `if`s, the `else`s and the conditions, we ended up with a piece of code that made a lot more sense to us. And when we were about to move on to something else, we made that last analysis: what makes it easier to understand now?

One thing went against our intuition: we had increased the nesting of the convoluted `if` statement (if you'd like to read the full story, you can find it here[3]). Usually, nesting is seen as a bad thing, so we were surprised that the more nested code turned out to be more expressive than the less nested one.

After some reflection, we put our finger on what *was* better in that new version of the `if` statement: it looked a lot like the specification coming from the business. Conversely, the previous version was more compact, but looked different

---

[3] https://www.fluentcpp.com/2017/07/21/making-if-statements-understandable/

from what the specification was asking for, even though it was logically equivalent.

We were then able to come up with this guideline: the most important characteristic we know to make an `if` statement understandable is to make it look like the specification. And this matters more than reducing nesting.

What this illustrates is that we should look back at our refactorings, find what we improved exactly, and extract a guideline from the context, so that it becomes applicable to any place in code. Doing that effectively augments our skills as software developers.

The vaccine analogy

There is a nice analogy that illustrates this way of analysing your (or anyone else's, for that matter) improvements of the code: it works like a **vaccine**.

Here is how a vaccine works: you inject a dose of a disease into your body, safe enough so that your body can beat it. It takes a few days for your immune system to figure it out, analyse exactly what the shape of the disease is like, and build a response to it. When the incident is over, your body **remembers it**.

Next time you face the same disease, even in its active form, its previous analysis and recording makes it manageable for your immune system to smash it apart before your being aware of it.

The same goes with bad code. The small dose of bad code you refactor is like the small dose of a virus that enters your system. Then the crucial part of analysis of the improvement of the code, and of remembering it, is like the immune system recording the shape of the attacker.

As a result, the next time you encounter the same type of bad code (in our case above, an intricate if statement), you know exactly what to look for. Like your immune system prevails over an attacking virus, you can smash apart a piece of bad code in no time, thanks to the careful analysis you took the time to do that first time.

And the more analyses like this you do, the more diverse the types of bad code you will be able to fix.

Be aware of what good code looks like

The above two techniques will let you learn plenty of things when you spend time in a legacy codebase, and improve your skills as a software developer. But at some point, also looking at good code also provides a useful complement. This is our third technique.

If you're used to looking at good code, **bad code stands out in contrast**. Knowing what good code resembles speeds up your analysis to locate what's wrong in bad code.

Sometimes, it may come down to gut feeling. Indeed, you won't find an improved version of your legacy code in the wild, but having your eyes used to elegant implementations and well-designed interfaces helps building an intuition.

In a legacy codebase, a lot of the code tends to be inspired, if not duplicated, from other parts of the same codebase. The members of one team or one company can copy each other, even if sometimes unconsciously. For that reason, getting some fresh air helps you realize there are other ways to go about designing a piece of code.

But if you only work in a legacy codebase, where can you find good code to look at? This is what we discuss in Chapter 3.

Key takeaways

- If you don't like a piece of code, think about the reason why.
- Explain to yourself the reason of your dislike in meticulous details.
- Write out your finding for your present self, you future self and for others.
- When you improve a piece of code, take a moment to think about why the new version is better.
- Consider using the vaccine analogy if you need to explain your meticulous approach to others.

Chapter 3: Why reading good code is important (and where to find it)

Some people believe that code is art. That crafting a piece of code is a work of art, and that readers of code appreciate the beauty of good code, like they would of a poem. Some books of our industry reflect this vision, such as *The Art of Computer Programming* or *Beautiful Code*.

I don't know if I'd go as far as code being poetry, but there is for sure an analogy between programming languages such as C++, Java, Python on one side, and human languages like English, French and Spanish on the other side.

One thing that all those languages have in common, computers and humans alike, is that they allow for several ways to express one given idea. Even a multitude of ways.

Those various ways have different trade-offs. Some are elegant but hard to understand and some are easy to understand only when you're used to them. Some are inelegant but go straight to the point. And some are both clumsy and hard to understand.

Chapter 3: Why reading good code is important (and where to find it)

Each language is a marvellous box of tools to combine in order to express your ideas to other humans. Amongst them, programming languages allow to express ideas not only to other humans, but also to computers.

Like a good writer masters the art of prose or poetry, being a good software developer requires mastering the craft of programming.

The importance of reading good code

There are ways to drastically improve your English (or, if you're not a native English speaker, to improve whichever your mother tongue is). One of those ways is to read good English (or good texts in your mother tongue).

If you consistently read books from authors such as Charles Dickens, Georges Orwell or Oscar Wilde, your English will improve. You will make far less spelling mistakes, acquire new vocabulary, and construct more elegant sentences. And sometimes this improvement will be automatic, operating in a subconscious way.

Using the analogy between programming languages and human languages, the translation is easy: one way to write better code is by reading good code.

Reading good code allows you to discover new ways to solve problems. It also makes you familiar with elegant style and, most importantly, it gives you a feeling for what abstractions work well.

Having a good intuition about what abstractions work well can have a lot of impact on how you design your own code. Indeed, a lot of what writing good code is about comes down to making proper use of abstraction levels, and deciding which abstractions to put in place is the first step to a good design.

Reading good code will show on your programming style and, as is the case with reading good English, the impact on the way you write code will sometimes happen unconsciously.

On top of influencing the way you write code, getting accustomed to reading good code can have an impact on the way you *read* programs: if your eyes are used to seeing good code, design issues stand out to you with more accuracy. This can help you apply some of the techniques we saw in Chapter 2 about using bad code to learn how to write great code.

And don't worry if not all the code you get to read is excellent. In his book *On Writing*, Stephen King advocates for reading a lot of good books, but also some less well-written books too, in order to know what to pursue as well as what to avoid.

Anyway, with a legacy codebase, I'm going to assume that you have not-so-good code at your disposal, perhaps even more than you wish you had.

But if you're working with such a legacy codebase, then where can you find good code to read?

Where to find good code

There turns out to be plenty of places within your reach where you can read good code.

Your standard library

Programming languages are typically composed of two parts: its core and its standard library.

The core includes the basic and fundamental blocks that constitute the language syntax. Typically, the primitive types (integer, floating point, character) as well as the building blocks for control flow (`if` statements, `for` loops) are part of the core.

The standard library comes along on top of this to add features that address generic needs: containers (list, map, array), operations on containers (sorting, partitioning), concurrency, serialization, and a plethora of components designed to make coding with that language easier.

When we learn a language, we typically learn a lot of the core, but we may not invest as much time to learn **how to use the standard library**. I guess it is because we can't do anything at all without the core, but without the library we can sort of get around, even if in a sub-optimal way.

However, knowing your standard library well is one of the most beneficial investments you can make as a software developer. And here I'm not talking about the how your standard library is implemented (although we'll come back to this in a moment), but rather what it offers to users of the language, and how to use it well.

For one thing, being aware of what is included in the standard library, and using it, makes your code simpler by saving you from re-inventing the wheel many times over. But studying code that uses the standard library also serves our purpose: it gives you a model of what good code looks like.

Indeed, the standard library was developed along with the rest of the language. This means that it should be well integrated with the idioms of the language.

Also, the standard library provides components that implement some abstractions. This means that they are the result of some choices about what abstractions to represent. As a result, being familiar with those components develops your instinct about how to choose which abstractions to introduce in your own code. An instinct that you can reuse for your own code.

Where to get some practice

Where can you find what the standard library offers? One place is the language documentation, but that can be a little hard to digest, in particular since standard libraries can be so vast.

Chapter 3: Why reading good code is important (and where to find it)

Another way to study the components provided by the standard library - but this time without falling asleep - is by reading code that uses them. This sort of code illustrates how library features fit well with the rest of the language.

So you should pay close attention whenever you see code that uses the standard library, whether it is in your legacy codebase or somewhere else.

But there is a trick that comes with that: how will you know if a given piece of code uses the standard library correctly? How to be sure that this piece of code is indeed good to get inspired from, and not something to run away from?

You need to be able to judge the quality of code that uses the standard library. And for this, two things can help: practice, and knowledge.

To acquire practice, you need to... practice. Concretely, this means striving to use the standard library when you have to modify your legacy codebase. What's nice about the standard library is that it comes natively with the language, so you shouldn't have to go through technical loops and installs to plug it in the codebase. It's already there.

Note that using the standard library in legacy code may not feel smooth at first. It takes time to look up the documentation, and the first trials are less than optimal. But over time you'll get better, and also acquire more acute judgement for whether the standard library is used correctly or not in a given piece of code.

Then the benefits of practice are amplified by knowledge.

There are plenty of ways you can acquire knowledge and share it, which we'll see in more detail in Chapters 8 and 9.

For the standard library, you could read a bit of documentation every day, or read dedicated resources about it. If you are a C++ developer, you can check out the STL Learning Resource[4] where I regularly write about what is in the C++ standard library, its use cases and its pitfalls.

Some parts that are hard to understand are special because they've been there for a long time, and don't benefit from as modern a design as the rest of the library. Don't worry too much about those, there are plenty of other places to explore in a standard library.

Your almost-standard library

During the course of its life, a language gets new features added to its standard library. Where do those features come from? Do they just appear to language maintainters to be pasted into the language specification?

Not really. They come out of tears, sweat, blood and experimentation time. Ok, maybe not out of sweat and blood, and hopefully not out of tears, but new features that end up in the language often go through some incubation somewhere.

Indeed, some languages have a large collection of libraries that are not officially standard, but that have a lot of expo-

---
[4] https://www.fluentcpp.com/STL

sure and contributors. For C++ for example, this would be the Boost libraries[5].

Those libraries are stimulating the innovation of the language. Their function is to complement the standard library and sometimes to explore and push the boundaries of the language.

Even if not every feature of those libraries ends up in the standard library, a lot of it is still worth knowing. They are typically peer-reviewed and have high-quality standards. They offer a lot of good code, interfaces and abstractions for you to read and get inspired from.

The next version of the language

Getting a library accepted in Boost is hard, but having it in the next version of C++ is even harder. This is why what is coming in the next version of your language, be there C++ or another programming language, is supposed to have gone under a lot of scrutiny.

Programming languages evolve, and reading about what is coming next in yours, along with code examples, gives you another opportunity to read good and modern code. You can read about how to use the new features, or go through their proposal papers that explain their rationale.

Moreover, it allows you to design code in a way that sets it in the same direction the language is taking, or at least

---

[5] https://www.boost.org

in a direction that doesn't contradict it. This is valuable even if you don't have the latest version in production yet (legacy codebases tend to have a hard time upgrading their infrastructure), because one day you will probably have it.

Open source projects

There is a ton of code out there in open source projects that you can read by just visiting their public repositories. But how to choose which ones to read?

If you follow the news related to the programming language you're interested in (by following blogs, videos, podcasts...), check out the code of the popular projects that everyone is talking about. Their code can contains a lot of valuable things to read.

Alternatively, you can have a look at the popular projects in your language of interest. To identify the popular projects, Github has a system of stars to upvote a repository, along with a trending projects page[6]. However, be careful because repositories are often upvoted for the usefulness of the application rather than for the quality of their code.

Libraries implementations

Once you get familiar with what your standard library has to offer, one possible next step is to look at what is inside, as in how it is implemented. Or to look at another library

---
[6] https://github.com/trending

that lets you write code that you love. On the top of seeing some quite polished code, you'll get a better intuition and understanding about the library as a whole.

But this step needs a bit of experience. If you peek inside and can't understand anything, just close it for now. What can make it hard to read is that it can be optimized for broad applicability (compiler compatibility, OS conformance, performance optimization...) rather than readability, and that it is tweaked to work on a lot of platforms.

You'll always have a chance to get back to it later, when time and practice have sharpened your code-reading skills.

Your legacy codebase

The purpose of this chapter was to point you to places where you can get some fresh air and read good code, but a legacy codebase can be full of surprises!

The code of a legacy codebase has been there for a long time, and layers of various epochs have sedimented over it. Some layers are quite recent, and can provide instructive reading material (and even some older parts could be well designed too, even if using earlier technologies). But how to locate them?

Isn't there one or several developers in your company that you admire for their technical skills? It could be your mentor that we talked about in Chapter 1, or it could be someone else. Either way, it is worth it to have a look at the code they write. In can be in the codebase itself, or it can be prototypes that they have written on the side, before trying to adapt them into the existing code.

Become more efficient with legacy code

As a final note, be careful to use your reading of good code as a means to make it easier to work with legacy code, and not the opposite. Don't let your familiarity with good code make you despise the code you get to work on, and keep in mind that most people don't work with ideal code. Use the insights of good code as a help, as described in Chapter 2 on how to use bad code to learn how to write great code.

Whichever source you decide to use, try to spend at least a bit of time to read good code on a regular basis. This will improve your skills as a software developer, give you some fresh air out of the legacy code, and provide you with more tools to tackle it efficiently.

Chapter 3: Why reading good code is important (and where to find it)

> **Key takeaways**
>
> - Take the time to read good code to improve your own code writing skills.
> - Search for good code in code that uses the standard library, big recognized libraries, the next version of your programming language, open source projects, library implementations, and your legacy codebase.
> - Use this to become more effective with your legacy codebase, not to blame it.

Part II: 10 techniques to understand legacy code

Chapter 4: 3 techniques to get an overview of the code
Chapter 5: 4 techniques to become a code speed-reader
Chapter 6: 3 techniques to understand code in detail

Chapter 4: 3 techniques to get an overview of the code

According to our definition in the introduction of this book, legacy code is, amongst other things, difficult to understand.

Chapter 1 helped you to adopt the right mindset towards legacy code. Now let's review several ways to tackle the code itself in order to figure out what it does.

If you find yourself struggling to understand legacy code, then applying the techniques of this part of the book will help you see through the code more clearly.

Let's start off with 3 techniques that will give you an overview of the code:

1. Choosing a stronghold
2. Starting from the inputs and outputs of the program (and how to find them)
3. Analysing well-chosen stacks

1) Choosing a stronghold

Think about those strategy games where you start with a little base and then you have to develop and explore the surroundings, which are blacked out when you start the game:

The partially uncovered map of a strategy game

When you start the game, the map of the world is almost entirely black, except for one thing: your base. Your base is a starting point for exploration. You can move around it and discover the surroundings to enlarge your vision of the world.

These games are a good comparison for a codebase: one

way to start the exploration of a part of a legacy codebase that you're interested in is to pick a place in the code that you understand very well (or at least, better than the rest of the code). This will be like your stronghold to start the game with. And don't worry about the size of this initial stronghold - even one line of code can be a starting point for exploration.

For example, one of the pieces of software I worked on performed various sorts of computations, one of them was very simple: a linear interpolation.

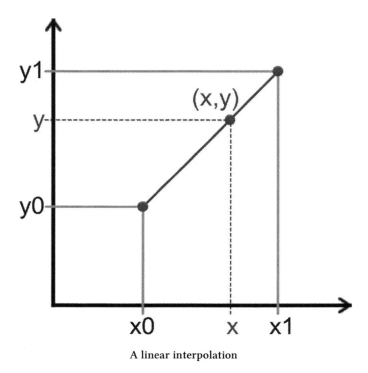

A linear interpolation

A linear interpolation consists in estimating a value between two known values, and its formula is relatively straightforward: y = y0 + (x - x0) * (y1 - y0) / (x1 - x0), which is independent from any software representation.

In that application I worked on, I had to get familiar with the code of a certain feature, and I knew that this feature had to perform a linear interpolation at some point. My goal was then to locate the code that implemented that linear implementation in order to create a first anchor in my mental representation of the code.

To locate the code of the feature to begin with, I started from the inputs and outputs of that feature in the application, as explained in technique 2) below. Then I began looking for code implementing the linear implementation in the codebase, by reading code and stepping through it with a debugger.

Plenty of things looked unfamiliar during that exploration of the code. But I looked for cues in function or class names that had a chance to be related to performing a computation, and then a linear interpolation, which could eventually drive me to its code.

When I finally encountered the linear interpolation, I had my stronghold. Since I understood it (by recognizing the above formula), it created an anchor point. I could start making mental connections between the surrounding code and this anchor point and understand the surrounding code as well.

The case of the linear interpolation is an example to illustrate what a stronghold can be, but in the general case it doesn't have to be a formula. To have a stronghold, you need to find a small unit or line of code that you understand perfectly in the context of the application.

Once you have found your stronghold, hold on to it. It constitutes a starting point from where to begin your exploration of the codebase. Indeed, chances are high that you also understand the line just before and the one just after your stronghold. And with a little more effort, you can probably figure out the immediate surroundings of those lines too.

Little by little, more and more code starts making sense. Little by little you will be expanding the area you're comfortable with, and the dark area on the map will start shrinking.

You can have more than one stronghold in the codebase. The more anchor points you have, the better you can understand the codebase.

Finding your stronghold can be challenging. If you are looking for a formula in a unfamiliar codebase of hundreds of thousands or millions of lines of code, it is like looking for a needle in a haystack.

The ideal situation is when you have access to someone who is already familiar with a part of the codebase, and who can point you to the code you are searching.

But if you're totally unfamiliar with the codebase, don't have access to a more experienced developer and don't know where to start to find a stronghold, technique 2) will help you get familiar with at least some places in the codebase on your own, by working your way from inputs and outputs. This will reduce the scope of code to search in, and make it easier to locate a piece of code that you understand well.

Once you have that reduced scope, explore it by reading the code or stepping through it with a debugger. Even if you don't understand all the code yet, focus on cues that look related to the unit you're after (which was the linear interpolation in the story above), until you get to its code.

A good stronghold needs to be specific. For instance, a function that puts a string in uppercase is not in itself a good stronghold, because it is typically used in several unrelated places across the codebase. Rather, some business code that calls this function in a context that you know in the application is a better stronghold.

Finding your stronghold and expanding from there is a very useful technique for getting oriented in unfamiliar source code. But at some point you have to push your knowledge way beyond your stronghold, particularly if your codebase has hundreds of thousands or millions of lines of code. Therefore, there are other techniques to complement this one and to discover more of that map faster.

2) Starting from the inputs and outputs of the program (and how to find them)

If you cannot recognize anything in the code and no one is there to explain it to you, there is still hope! Often, you can at least find someone who is familiar with the application itself from a user point of view, if not with the code.

Ask that person for a common use case with the application and to show you how it works in the Graphical User

Interface (or any other form of input and output of the application). And if you can't access anyone who can tell you about a common use case, look for a piece of documentation, blog post, tutorial, readme, etc. to find out.

The code must somehow take inputs from and produce outputs to that interface. Find where this input comes into the code. Resort to grepping for any name that shows in the interfaces if you cannot find them otherwise.

Once you have found a trace of the UI input or output in the code, follow it like a thread until you reach the code of the test case that the business person showed you. Even if this feature boils down to just one line of code. This will be your stronghold, and then you can apply technique 1) above and start out from there.

To be able to work your way from the UI layer to the corresponding business code, you'll need to have some familiarity with the UI framework of your application. Investing time in understanding it will pay off dozens of time over.

You don't need to understand every last piece of the UI framework, but spend at least once a few hours studying how information is carried from graphical events to business code and back. This will help you locate the code corresponding to the features of your application.

There is another source of inputs and outputs than the UI: **tests**! Tests, just like UI, trigger the execution of the code of the application by sending it inputs and collecting outputs from it (and checking that these outputs are as expected).

But most tests - all except system tests - are closer to the code than the UI, as they call an inner portion of the code. If you are trying to figure out a piece of code that is buried deep in the codebase, a long way from the UI, a test around it can provide a shortcut to reach it with inputs and outputs more easily.

3) Analysing well-chosen stacks

Another way to take a step back on a part of the codebase is to look at a call stack. The idea here is to fire up the debugger, find a "judicious" place in the code where to put a breakpoint, and launch a use case in the application.

What kind of breakpoint is "judicious"? One that is **deep in a stack of a typical use case** of the application.

If you don't know what use case is typical in the application, it can help to sit with your manager (or someone else who is familiar with the architecture of the application) so that they can pick one for you and show where to set that breakpoint. Or if you are the one who knows, sit down with the developers you are mentoring to apply this technique.

If there is no developer around you that is familiar with the architecture of the application, go back again to technique 2) to locate a place you can become familiar with.

Once you have launched the application and the breakpoint has been hit, look at the call stack. It displays in one shot all the layers of the application involved in that use case.

That sort of snapshot provides insights on the architecture of your software: what the main modules and the frameworks are and how they relate together. A call stack tells a long story[7].

Do not do this exercise only once. It would be like going on a safari and taking only one picture. Repeat this experiment for several call stacks in the same use case in order to get a grasp of the sequencing of the calls, and repeat the process for other typical use cases of the application.

Debuggers allow you to navigate up and down the stack. And doing this allows to see the code surrounding each call in the stack and to understand which path the application took to reach this breakpoint. Then, executing the code line by line or stepping up and continuing tracing the code is helpful in understanding how the code behaves in this typical use-case.

Flame graphs

Flame graphs are a way to visualize several call stacks at the same time. They aggregate the data produced by a performance analysis tool (such as `perf` on Linux) into a picture representing the stacks that a program went through during its execution.

---

[7] Some debuggers display the module name for each function in the call stack. For example, Microsoft Visual Studio does it if you do Right click > "Show module name" on the call stack. This lets you see how modules interact together on a given use case.

The breadth of a given call stack is proportional to its frequency of occurrence. Thus flame graphs allow to identify the large stacks that stand out of the picture as the ones where the program spends most of its time. The primary purpose of flame graphs is performance analysis.

But leaving the performance aspects aside, a flamegraph allows to see several call stacks of our program and to navigate in them. For example, the flame graphs generated with Brendan Gregg's tools[8] are interactive SVG files.

Here is an example of a flame graph that shows the execution of a program:

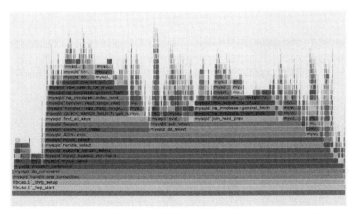

MySQL CPU Flame Graph (Courtesy of Brendan Gregg)

In a flamegraph, identical call stacks are lumped together to form the blocks displayed in the picture. This has several consequences on how to read the picture to get an overview

---

[8]http://www.brendangregg.com/flamegraphs.html

of the code.

First, you don't choose the stacks to display: the prominents blocks are those were the program spends a good proportion of its time. However, if a lot of time is spent in a stack, it may play an important role in the program and be interesting to observe.

Note though that you can zoom in on a particular block of the flamegraph. In this example, if we'd like to see more details on the stack stemming from the SQL_SE-LECT::skip_record, we can hover the mouse on it:

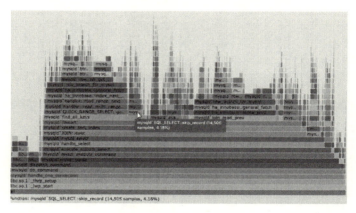

And click to expand that part of the graph:

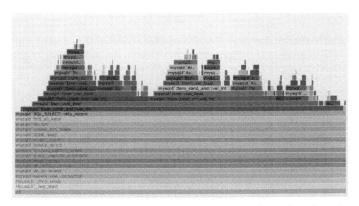

Zoom on SQL_SELECT::skip_record (Courtesy of Brendan Gregg)

So even if a particular function is not amongst the most representative of the program execution time, you can still zoom in on it to display a flame graph focused on the stacks stemming from that function (or rather, stemming from the bottom of the stack that led to that function).

Another thing to note is that the horizontal axis does not represent points in time. This means that stacks are not displayed in their order of appearance (in Brendan Gregg's flame graphs, stacks are sorted by alphabetical order). It makes sense because several identical stacks appearing at different times are lumped together into a block.

This means that a flamegraph doesn't tell a chronological story of what happened during the execution. It only brings out a set of representative (in terms of frequency) stacks that were called by the program.

There are other tools that Brendan Gregg's to build flame

70 Chapter 4: 3 techniques to get an overview of the code

graphs out of the stack of a program. For instance the Windows Performance Analyzer (WPA) also allows to visualize flame graphs:

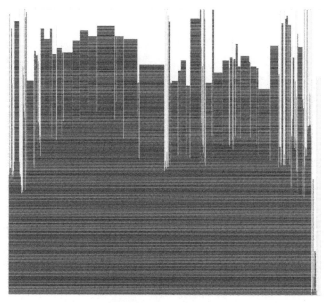

A WPA flame graph

A good starting point to build flame graphs with WPA are the tutorials on Bruce Dawson's blog[9].

I found WPA flame graphs less easy to navigate: they display function names only when zooming very close (otherwise function names appear only when hovering

---

[9]https://randomascii.wordpress.com/2016/09/05/etw-flame-graphs-made-easy/

the mouse), and you are not allowed to scroll inside of the flame graph, which makes big graphs impractical to navigate.

In your exploration of the codebase, you will come across pieces of code you need to understand. The coming chapters show how to interpret such pieces of code and quickly figure out what they are about.

> **Key takeaways**
>
> - Locate a piece (or even line) of code you can map to something you understand in the application. Then relate the surrounding code to it.
> - Get familiar with your UI framework, to travel from the UI to the code and back.
> - Analyze call stacks that are both deep and in a representative test case of the application.
> - Flamegraphs can display several call stacks at the same time.

Chapter 5: 4 techniques to become a code speed-reader

How to read a book? If it's a fiction book, chances are you are reading it to have a good time. In this case reading it linearly, line by line and cover to cover, is what makes the most sense.

But in the case of non-fiction books, you are reading to acquire knowledge and understanding. And as explained in the classic *How to read a book* from M. Adler and C. Von Doren, you do not want to read such books cover to cover. Rather, you want to start with an "inspectional reading".

An inspectional reading consists in skimming through the book, looking for places that sum up the information (table of contents, beginning and end of chapters, main messages...). Inspectional reading is *fast*. This skimming of the book allows to achieve two things:

- decide whether this book is indeed relevant for you,
- get an idea of the main message and parts of the book.

Going back to source code, what sort of book do you think source code relates to the most: fiction, or non-fiction?

Unless you are fond enough of a piece of code to enjoy reading it like you would read a good novel, source code is a read for knowledge and understanding. Like non-fiction books.

For this reason you do not want to start by reading a function "cover to cover", that is going through its code line after line starting from the first and going all the way to the last. Instead you want to skim over lines of code, looking for the main information. You want to perform an inspectional reading on code for the same two reasons as for a book:

- deciding whether this piece of code is relevant for you and deserves a deeper analysis,
- getting a general idea of its meaning before getting into the details.

And only when you have performed the inspectional reading should you read the book in more detail to get the entirety of the message from the author.

The techniques that follow will show you how to extract the relevant information during the inspectional reading of a function:

1. Working your way backwards from the function's outputs
2. Identifying the terms that occur frequently
3. Filtering on control flow
4. Distinguishing the main action of the function

1) Working your way backwards from the function's outputs

Before delving into its implementation, the first thing to look at is the function's name. If it is well named, it should give a general understanding of what it does and orient you for what to look for when you inspect its body.

Or better yet, the name, parameters and return type should be enough to indicate everything you need to know about this function.

However, not all functions are created equal, and some of them require you to get a peek under the hood. Or sometimes, it feels more like a descent deep into a cave.

When you're inside the cave, what should you start looking for? The first thing to look inside a function is **its output**. All the rest of the function is oriented towards producing that output (or the set of outputs—more on this in a moment), because it's the purpose of the function.

For example, for a function that returns a value, get a big spoiler, skip to the end of that function's story, and start from the last line. It can look like `return something`. In this case, this `something` is what the function is built around.

Knowing that all its code is oriented towards producing that `something` will help you understand the function. But maybe you won't even have to: knowing what the goal of a function is often brings enough information, for example if you are reading this function to understand another place in the code that calls it.

Some functions have multiple return statements. If that is the case, look at all of them and try to see what they have in common to get a feeling of what that function is returning.

Some functions don't even return values and perform side effects such as modifying their parameters or, for object methods, modifying the state of the object. That counts as "outputs" too.

Some functions go as far as modifying global variables, and some even return values via exceptions, even though this is not a good practice. All the side effects of a function count as its outputs (which is why you want to avoid side effects in a function in order to make it simpler). Anyway, however unfortunate the form of the output, this is what you should be looking for first.

Let's look at a piece of code to illustrate this technique. Below is a function from an open source project called igv, coded in Java, which I copied from GitHub. This project allows to analyse genetic data. The point is not to pick on that particular project, but rather to see how to make some sense out of a piece of code that we don't know.

Here is a function extracted from that project:

```java
public List<MultipleAlignmentBlock> loadAlignments(String chr,
int start, int end) throws IOException {

    IntervalTree ivTree = index.getIntervalTree(chr);
    if (ivTree == null) return null;

    List<Interval> intervals = ivTree.findOverlapping(start, end);
    if (intervals.isEmpty()) {
        return null;
    }

    // Find the starting (left most) interval.  Alignment blocks
    // do not overlap, so we can start at the minimum file
    // offset and just proceed until the end of the interval.
    long startPosition = Long.MAX_VALUE;
    for (Interval iv : intervals) {
        startPosition = Math.min(startPosition, iv.getValue());
    }

    SeekableStream is = null;

    is=IGVSeekableStreamFactory.getInstance().getStreamFor(path);
    is.seek(startPosition);

    BufferedReader reader =
        new BufferedReader(new InputStreamReader(is), 256000);

    List<MultipleAlignmentBlock> alignments =
        new ArrayList<MultipleAlignmentBlock>();

    String line;
    while ((line = reader.readLine()) != null) {
        if (line.startsWith("a ")) {
            // TODO -- parse score (optional)
            MultipleAlignmentBlock block = parseBlock(reader);
            if(block.getEnd() < start) {
                continue;
            }
```

78 Chapter 5: 4 techniques to become a code speed-reader

```
39              if (block.getStart() > end || !block.getChr().equals(\
40   chr)) {
41                  break;
42              } else {
43                  alignments.add(block);
44              }
45          }
46      }
47      return alignments;
48  }
```

Even if we don't know anything about the codebase that this function belongs to, we can understand its purpose and basic structure by applying the techniques presented in this chapter.

For instance, this function returns an object, `alignments` on line 47. This is therefore the main character of the function (which makes sense, given the name of the function: `loadAlignments`). We can therefore assume that the whole direction of the function is to construct those `alignments`.

A quick look at the other `return` statements in the function (lines 5 and 9) just show that they seem to deal with corner cases (they return `null`) and do not participate in the main goal of the function.

The only object that interacts with `alignments` is `block` (line 43). `block` is therefore interesting to follow. `block` is in turn constructed from `reader` (line 35), which comes from the first half of the function.

Note how those few observations quickly gave us an overall view of the function: the first half is about setting up a reader, which is used in the second half to construct the alignments with intermediaries objects, the blocks. We can consider that the "output" of the first half of the function is the reader that is then used as one "input" of the second half of the function. Identifying such "inputs" and "outputs" inside the body of a function helps to understand the function and we can take advantage of this information to refactor the code as explained in technique 2) of Chapter 6.

We now have the first half of the function left to understand. Since this part of the function is farther away from the main character alignments, we will use another technique to analyse it: identifying the terms that occur frequently.

2) Identifying the terms that occur frequently

Looking for outputs in the general sense is a good starting point because they are the main characters of the function. But in some cases the outputs don't show easily, like in the case of side effects hiding in sub-functions called by the function you're examining.

If you cannot find the main characters of the function by looking at the outputs, another approach is to look for **the objects that appear the most frequently in its code**. Indeed, if they appear often then they probably play a central role in it. Focusing on what is happening to the objects that come up often in code allows to get a better idea of what the code is doing.

Note that this technique is also useful when you are only inspecting a portion of a larger function, as opposed to a function as a whole. If nothing gets returned in that portion, identifying the objects that appear the most often helps identifying what that portion of code is about.

Once you have identified the objects that occur the most frequently, highlighting them in any IDE[10] reveals patterns. Carefully chosen, these patterns can provide useful information and a high level view of a piece of code. We will now see this technique applied in several examples.

Locating the important objects

To illustrate how highlighting the frequent terms can help understanding a piece of code, we will identify and locate the terms occurring the most frequently in the code of another open-source project, Classic-Shell, coded in C++ this time. We start with a function called `ReadValue`. I include it here for later reference in the chapter. You don't have to read it line by line now, because the very purpose of our analysis is to start with a big picture of the function.

---

[10]Integrated Development Environment

```cpp
bool CSetting::ReadValue(CRegKey &regKey, const wchar_t *valName)
{
    // bool, int, hotkey, color
    if (type==CSetting::TYPE_BOOL
        || (type==CSetting::TYPE_INT
            && this[1].type!=CSetting::TYPE_RADIO)
        || type==CSetting::TYPE_HOTKEY
        || type==CSetting::TYPE_HOTKEY_ANY
        || type==CSetting::TYPE_COLOR)
    {
        DWORD val;
        if (regKey.QueryDWORDValue(valName,val)==ERROR_SUCCESS)
        {
            if (type==CSetting::TYPE_BOOL)
                value=CComVariant(val?1:0);
            else
                value=CComVariant((int)val);
            return true;
        }
        return false;
    }

    // radio
    if (type==CSetting::TYPE_INT
        && this[1].type==CSetting::TYPE_RADIO)
    {
        ULONG len;
        DWORD val;
        if (regKey.QueryStringValue(valName,NULL,&len)==ERROR_SUCCESS)
        {
            CString text;
            regKey.QueryStringValue(valName,text.GetBuffer(len),&len);
            text.ReleaseBuffer(len);
            val=0;
            for (const CSetting *pRadio=this+1;
                    pRadio->type==CSetting::TYPE_RADIO;pRadio++,val++)
            {
                if (_wcsicmp(text,pRadio->name)==0)
```

```
39        {
40           value=CComVariant((int)val);
41           return true;
42        }
43      }
44    }
45    else if (regKey.QueryDWORDValue(valName,val)==ERROR_SUCCESS)
46    {
47      value=CComVariant((int)val);
48      return true;
49    }
50    return false;
51  }
52
53  // string
54  if (type>=CSetting::TYPE_STRING
55        && type<CSetting::TYPE_MULTISTRING)
56  {
57    ULONG len;
58    if (regKey.QueryStringValue(valName,NULL,&len)==ERROR_SUCCESS)
59    {
60      value.vt=VT_BSTR;
61      value.bstrVal=SysAllocStringLen(NULL,len-1);
62      regKey.QueryStringValue(valName,value.bstrVal,&len);
63      return true;
64    }
65    return false;
66  }
67
68  // multistring
69  if (type==CSetting::TYPE_MULTISTRING)
70  {
71    ULONG len;
72    if (regKey.QueryMultiStringValue(valName,NULL,&len)==ERROR_SU\
73  CCESS)
74    {
75      value.vt=VT_BSTR;
76      value.bstrVal=SysAllocStringLen(NULL,len-1);
```

```
77          regKey.QueryMultiStringValue(valName,value.bstrVal,&len);
78          for (int i=0;i<(int)len-1;i++)
79            if (value.bstrVal[i]==0)
80              value.bstrVal[i]='\n';
81          return true;
82        }
83        else if (regKey.QueryStringValue(valName,NULL,&len)==ERROR_SU\
84   CCESS)
85        {
86          value.vt=VT_BSTR;
87          value.bstrVal=SysAllocStringLen(NULL,len);
88          regKey.QueryStringValue(valName,value.bstrVal,&len);
89          if (len>0)
90          {
91            value.bstrVal[len-1]='\n';
92            value.bstrVal[len]=0;
93          }
94          return true;
95        }
96        return false;
97      }
98
99      Assert(0);
100     return false;
101   }
```

On its last line, the function returns a boolean. For such a big function, this boolean probably means that the function succeeded or failed, but this is probably not the real output of the function. We need to search for the real output.

Let's see which terms come up the most frequently in the above function. To achieve this, we can either scan the function and get a feel for words we see frequently or, for longer pieces of code, use a tool to do this for us.

Here we will use the online word counter available on

Fluent C++[11]. Its output for this function starts with this:

Word	#	span	proportion
len	20	64	64.65%
value	17	76	76.77%
CSetting	15	69	69.7%
if	14	84	84.85%
type	13	66	66.67%
regKey	11	86	86.87%
valName	11	86	86.87%
return	11	81	81.82%

Let's look at the second column of this output (we will explore the other columns in Chapter 13 on how to reduce the size of long functions). It indicates number of occurrences of a given word.

As we can see, one of the words occurring the most frequently in this function is value. When highlighting the occurrences of value in the code, here is the patterns that comes out:

---

[11] http://www.fluentcpp.com/word-count/

The first thing we can note is that the occurrences of value are spread out across the whole function. This suggests that value is indeed an central object of the function. Note that if we had started by reading the code line by line, it would have taken much more time to figure out this piece of information.

We also note that the first time that `value` appears in the function is not via a declaration (look at line 15 in the reference of the function a few pages back). This means that `value` is presumably a member of the class containing the method `ReadValue` (in theory `value` could also be a global variable; a quick check in the IDE would determine this).

Now if we have a closer look at those occurrences of `value` (lines 15, 17, 40, 47, 60, 61, 62, 75, 76, 77, 79, 80, 86, 87, 88, 91 and 92), we notice that most of them are assignments, and that most of those assignments are followed by a return statement.

We now have a good assumption about the purpose of the function `ReadValue`: filling the class member `value` (and we also understand the function's name now).

All these deductions are only based on assumptions, and to be 100% sure they are valid we would have to read the function in more detail.

But having a plausible explanation of what the function does is useful for two reasons:

- it is too time-consuming to read every last line of every function we come across,
- for the functions that we do end up reading in detail, starting with a general idea of what the function does helps the detailed reading.

Understanding how inputs are used

Since a function takes inputs and produces outputs, one way to understand it is also to examine what it does with its inputs. On several word counts I ran, the function's inputs were indeed amongst the most frequently appearing words in its body. We will now look at the occurrences of the inputs of the ReadValue function in its code.

The ReadValue function takes two inputs: regKey and valName. We highlight the occurrences of those words in the function. regKey is in the left highlighted column, valName in the right highlighted column:

88 Chapter 5: 4 techniques to become a code speed-reader

A pattern jumps out of this highlighting: regKey and valName are always used together. This suggests that, to understand them, we should consider them together. And indeed, by looking more closely at one of the lines where they are used, we see that regKey seems to be some sort of container, and valName a key to search into it.

Sometimes the input parameters are not used extensively in the function though. For example, consider this other function, SetIatHook, taken from the same codebase:

```
IatHookData *SetIatHook(IMAGE_DOS_HEADER *dosHeader,
DWORD iatOffset, DWORD intOfset, const char *targetProc,
void *newProc)
{
   IMAGE_THUNK_DATA *thunk=
      (IMAGE_THUNK_DATA*) PtrFromRva(dosHeader,iatOffset);
   IMAGE_THUNK_DATA *origThunk=
      (IMAGE_THUNK_DATA*) PtrFromRva(dosHeader,intOfset);
   for (;origThunk->u1.Function;origThunk++,thunk++)
   {
      if (origThunk->u1.Ordinal&IMAGE_ORDINAL_FLAG)
      {
         if (IS_INTRESOURCE(targetProc) &&
            IMAGE_ORDINAL(origThunk->u1.Ordinal)==(WORD)targetProc)
            break;
      }
      else
      {
         IMAGE_IMPORT_BY_NAME *import=(IMAGE_IMPORT_BY_NAME*)PtrFrom\
Rva(dosHeader,origThunk->u1.AddressOfData);
         if (!IS_INTRESOURCE(targetProc)
            && strcmp(targetProc,(char*)import->Name)==0)
            break;
      }
   }
   if (origThunk->u1.Function)
   {
      IatHookData *hook=g_IatHooks+g_IatHookCount;
      g_IatHookCount++;
      hook->jump[0]=hook->jump[1]=0x90; // NOP
      hook->jump[2]=0xFF; hook->jump[3]=0x25; // JUMP
```

Chapter 5: 4 techniques to become a code speed-reader

```
32  #ifdef __WIN64
33      hook->jumpOffs=0;
34  #else
35      hook->jumpOffs=(DWORD)(hook)+8;
36  #endif
37      hook->newProc=newProc;
38      hook->oldProc=(void*)thunk->u1.Function;
39      hook->thunk=thunk;
40      DWORD oldProtect;
41      VirtualProtect(&thunk->u1.Function,
42          sizeof(void*),PAGE_READWRITE,&oldProtect);
43      thunk->u1.Function=(DWORD_PTR)hook;
44      VirtualProtect(&thunk->u1.Function,
45          sizeof(void*),oldProtect,&oldProtect);
46      return hook;
47    }
48    return NULL;
49  }
```

In this function, the input parameter iatOffset is used only once:

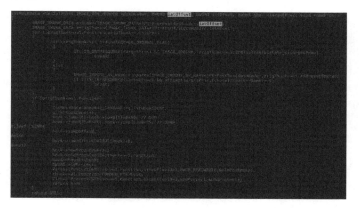

The input parameters iatOffset and intOfSet are used to

get some objects using the other dosHeader input at the very beginning of the function: thunk and origThunk. In such a case, it may be interesting to consider the resulting objects as the real inputs, highlight them and see how they are used:

In this case, the upper part of the function uses origThunk and the lower part only thunk.

In any case, it is always interesting to see where a function uses its inputs. After all, they constitute its starting point to perform its job.

Intensive uses of an object

Another pattern that comes up and that provides valuable information about a piece of code is the intensive use of a word in a portion of the code, and very few usages outside of this portion. This suggests that this portion of code is focused on using a particular object, which can clarify the responsibilities of the portion of code.

To illustrate this, let's consider the example of the `ParseTreeSec` function in the Classic-Shell project:

```
1   int CSettingsParser::ParseTreeRec(const wchar_t *str,
2   std::vector<TreeItem> &items, CString *names, int level )
3   {
4       size_t start=items.size();
5       while (*str)
6       {
7           wchar_t token[256];
8           str=GetToken(str,token,_countof(token),L" ,\t");
9           if (token[0])
10          {
11              //
12              bool bFound=false;
13              for (int i=0;i<level;i++)
14                  if (_wcsicmp(token,names[i])==0)
15                  {
16                      bFound=true;
17                      break;
18                  }
19              if (!bFound)
20              {
21                  TreeItem item={token,-1};
22                  items.push_back(item);
23              }
24          }
25      }
26      size_t end=items.size();
27      if (start==end) return -1;
28
29      TreeItem item={L"",-1};
30      items.push_back(item);
31
32      if (level<MAX_TREE_LEVEL-1)
```

```
33      {
34          for (size_t i=start;i<end;i++)
35          {
36              wchar_t buf[266];
37              Sprintf(buf,_countof(buf),L"%s.Items",items[i].name);
38              const wchar_t *str2=FindSetting(buf);
39              if (str2)
40              {
41                  names[level]=items[i].name;
42              // these two statements must be on separate lines.
43              // otherwise items[i] is evaluated before ParseTreeRec, but
44              // the items vector can be reallocated inside ParseTreeRec,
45              // causing the address to be invalidated -> crash!
46                  int idx=ParseTreeRec(str2,items,names,level+1);
47                  items[i].children=idx;
48              }
49          }
50      }
51      return (int)start;
52  }
```

Running a word count shows that one of the terms that comes up frequently in this function is token. Let's see the visual pattern drawn by highlighting the occurrences of this term in the function's code:

94 Chapter 5: 4 techniques to become a code speed-reader

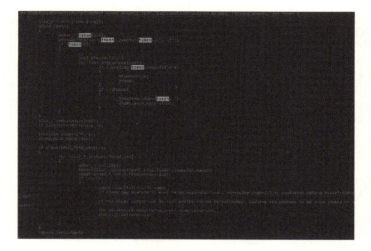

Since token appears many times in the while loop (on lines 7, 8, 9, 14 and 21), it suggests that it has a central role in that loop. This is reinforced by the fact that the first thing done in the loop is a call to GetToken, which name tells that it is used to set the value of token and that the rest of the loop is done conditionally on token[0].

This is good to know if we need to understand what the loop does, and it also suggests a refactoring idea: putting some of the body of the loop in a function that takes token as an input parameter, or refactor the whole loop into a separate function and fully get rid of the token variable in this ParseTreeRec function.

Continuing the analysis of `loadAlignments`

Let's apply the technique of locating frequent words to continue the analysis of the `loadAlignments` function seen earlier, by looking at its upper half:

```
1   public List<MultipleAlignmentBlock> loadAlignments(String chr,
2   int start, int end) throws IOException {
3
4       IntervalTree ivTree = index.getIntervalTree(chr);
5       if (ivTree == null) return null;
6
7       List<Interval> intervals = ivTree.findOverlapping(start, end);
8       if (intervals.isEmpty()) {
9           return null;
10      }
11
12      // Find the starting (left most) interval.  Alignment blocks
13      // do not overlap, so we can start at the minimum file
14      // offset and just proceed until the end of the interval.
15      long startPosition = Long.MAX_VALUE;
16      for (Interval iv : intervals) {
17          startPosition = Math.min(startPosition, iv.getValue());
18      }
19
20      SeekableStream is = null;
21
22      is=IGVSeekableStreamFactory.getInstance().getStreamFor(path);
23      is.seek(startPosition);
24
25      BufferedReader reader =
26          new BufferedReader(new InputStreamReader(is), 256000);
27
28
29      ...
```

A word count shows that a term occurring frequently in this piece of code is "interval". It appears in objects ("interval", "intervals", "iv"), in types ("Interval", "IntervalTree") as well as in comments. This piece of code is therefore presumably centered around the concept of intervals.

Without looking for the terms that occur frequently, we could have started by reading the function linearly, starting with its parameters: `chr, start` and `end`. Even if they are connected to the concept of an interval, they are lower in terms of levels of abstraction and make it harder to see the big picture.

We now know that this first part of the function works with a set of intervals, and works out a position based on them to create a `reader` on line 25, used in the second half of the function as we saw before in technique 1).

This is the skeleton of the function, which could be enough for a first analysis. If we want to know more details about a particular part of the function, we now know where to find them.

Combining techniques

To get more practice of the techniques seen so far, let's perform the analysis of another function from the igv project, that offers perhaps a little more of a challenge:

```
1   public synchronized void processAlignments(String chr,
2   List<Alignment> alignments) {
3
4     Genome genome = GenomeManager.getInstance().getCurrentGenome();
5     chr = genome == null ? chr : genome.getCanonicalChrName(chr);
6
7     Map<Integer,InsertionMarker> insertionMap=insertionMaps.get(chr);
8     if(insertionMap == null) {
9       insertionMap = Collections.synchronizedMap(new HashMap<>());
10      insertionMaps.put(chr, insertionMap);
11    }
12    List<Integer> positions = positionsMap.get(chr);
13    if(positions == null) {
14      positions = new ArrayList<>();
15      positionsMap.put(chr, positions);
16    }
17
18    int minLength = 0;
19    if (PreferencesManager.getPreferences().getAsBoolean(SAM_HIDE_S\
20  MALL_INDEL)) {
21      minLength = PreferencesManager.getPreferences().getAsInt(SAM_\
22  SMALL_INDEL_BP_THRESHOLD);
23    }
24
25    for (Alignment a : alignments) {
26      AlignmentBlock[] blocks = a.getInsertions();
27      if (blocks != null) {
28        for (AlignmentBlock block : blocks) {
29
30          if (block.getBases().length < minLength) continue;
31
32          Integer key = block.getStart();
33          InsertionMarker insertionMarker = insertionMap.get(key);
34          if (insertionMarker == null) {
35            insertionMarker = new InsertionMarker(
36                    block.getStart(), block.getLength());
37            insertionMap.put(key, insertionMarker);
38            positions.add(block.getStart());
```

```
39              } else {
40                  insertionMarker.size =
41                      Math.max(insertionMarker.size, block.getLength());
42              }
43          }
44      }
45  }
46
47
48      positions.addAll(insertionMap.keySet());
49      positions.sort((o1, o2) -> o1 - o2);
50  }
```

We could start our analysis from the outputs of the function, but this function doesn't show its outputs explicitly, as it returns `void`. Its name, `processAlignments`, suggests that its inputs are `alignments` but doesn't give any indication about the nature of the outputs.

Since the whole body of the function must be there to do something, we can try to glean some information about its outputs by looking towards its end:

```
1       positions.addAll(insertionMap.keySet());
2       positions.sort((o1, o2) -> o1 - o2);
3   }
```

Maybe the purpose of the function is to construct the object `positions`. Let's remember that hypothesis for later.

Let's look at the frequent terms to get an overview of the function secondary characters. A word count show that amongst the most frequent terms is `chr`. Here is the visual pattern drawn by highlighting the occurrences of `chr`:

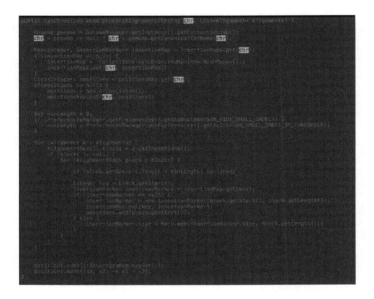

All the occurrences of chr appear in the first 14 lines of the function. This suggests the beginning of the function deals with the processing of chr.

Another term that comes up often is insertionMap. This term appears throughout the function:

100Chapter 5: 4 techniques to become a code speed-reader

insertionMap is looked up based on chr and created if not found. It is then used later in the function.

block also appears frequently, but all of its occurrences are located in the second half of the function. It comes from the alignments (remember that alignments were built from blocks in loadAlignments) that are used to populate insertionMap and positions. Finally, positions is also filled from insertionMap.

By hopping from one frequently occurring word to the other, we have reconstituted the story of the function: chr gives access to insertionMap and positions, which are filled with the blocks coming from alignments. This confirms our initial hypothesis that positions is an output of the function. However, it turned out that it wasn't the only one as insertionMap is also filled:

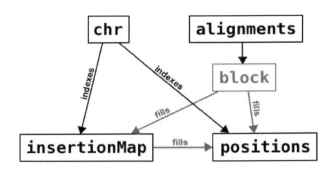

This quick analysis outlined the structure of the function. This indicates what this function does. If we need to know the details of how a given part is executed, we can use this structure as a map of the function to locate what to look for.

If applying techniques 1) and 2) doesn't provide enough indications of what a function is doing, technique 3) will help you cut through its code to get an overview of its structure.

3) Filtering on control flow

Best practices of writing code, such as those described in Bob Martins' book *Clean Code*, recommend to keep functions short. But in legacy code, this recommendation is not always respected in practice.

Reading long functions can be challenging. A function that is several hundreds or even thousands of lines long makes it hard to take a step back and understand what it is doing as a whole.

One way to instantly squeeze a long the function into a few lines of code is to filter on its control flow keywords: `if`, `else`, `for`, `while`, `switch`, `case`, `try`, `catch`, and so on. That is to say to hide all the lines of the function except those that contain the control flow keywords (that vary depending on the language).

Doing this exhibits the structure of the function, and in some cases gives an overview of the topics that the function treats and their order of appearance, indicating the general direction of the function.

It doesn't show exactly what the function does, because the lines containing the control flow keywords generally don't perform any action, but it shows the skeleton of the function. It is like getting a **table of contents** of the function.

Just like analyzing the table of contents of a book before diving into detailed reading allows to understand how each part relates to the whole, having an (even rough) idea of the structure of the function helps when reading it later.

Another thing that reading the table of contents of a book provides is the confirmation that you are on the right path because the book seems to contain information of interest. Or on the contrary that the information that the book is not for you in the end, because it doesn't seem to address the kind of topics you're after.

Let's illustrate this with an example. The following C++ function comes from an open source project called Scene-text-recognition[12]. The point is not to pick on that particular project, but rather to look at code we're not familiar with. Indeed, the following function is not trivial to read just by glancing at it:

```
ER* ERFilter::er_tree_extract(Mat input)
{
    CV_Assert(input.type() == CV_8UC1);

    Mat input_clone = input.clone();
    const int width = input_clone.cols;
    const int height = input_clone.rows;
    const int highest_level = (255 / THRESH_STEP) + 1;
    const uchar *imgData = input_clone.data;

    input_clone /= THRESH_STEP;

    //!< 1. Clear the accessible pixel mask, the heap of boundary
    //!<    pixels and the component
    bool *pixel_accessible = new bool[height*width]();
    vector<int> boundary_pixel[256];
    vector<int> boundary_edge[256];
    vector<ER *>er_stack;

    int priority = highest_level;


```

[12]https://github.com/HsiehYiChia/Scene-text-recognition

```
23      //!< 1-2. push a dummy-component onto the stack,
24      //!<    with grey-level heigher than any allowed in the image
25      er_stack.push_back(new ER(256, 0, 0, 0));
26
27
28      //!< 2. make the top-right corner the source pixel, get its
29      //!<    gray level and mark it accessible
30      int current_pixel = 0;
31      int current_edge = 0;
32      int current_level = imgData[current_pixel];
33      pixel_accessible[current_pixel] = true;
34
35
36  step_3:
37      int x = current_pixel % width;
38      int y = current_pixel / width;
39
40      //!< 3. push an empty component with current_level onto the
41      //!<    component stack
42      er_stack.push_back(new ER(current_level, current_pixel, x, y));
43
44
45      for (;;)
46      {
47        //!< 4. Explore the remaining edges to the neighbors of the
48        //!<    current pixel, in order, as follows :
49        //!<    For each neighbor, check if the neighbor is already
50        //!<    accessible.If it is not, mark it as accessible and
51        //!<    retrieve its grey - level.If the grey - level is not
52        //!<    lower than the current one, push it onto the heap of
53        //!<    boundary pixels.If on the other hand the grey - level
54        //!<    is lower than the current one, enter the current
55        //!<    pixel back into the queue of boundary pixels for later
56        //!<    processing(with the next edge number), consider the new
57        //!<    pixel and its grey - level and go to 3.
58        int neighbor_pixel;
59        int neighbor_level;
60
```

```
     for (; current_edge < 4; current_edge++)
     {
        switch (current_edge)
        {
           case right  : neighbor_pixel = (x + 1 < width)  ? curren\
t_pixel + 1     : current_pixel;  break;
           case bottom : neighbor_pixel = (y + 1 < height) ? curren\
t_pixel + width : current_pixel;  break;
           case left   : neighbor_pixel = (x > 0)          ? current_pix\
el - 1    : current_pixel;  break;
           case top    : neighbor_pixel = (y > 0)          ? current_pixel\
 - width  : current_pixel;  break;
           default: break;
        }

        if (!pixel_accessible[neighbor_pixel] && neighbor_pixel != \
current_pixel)
        {
           pixel_accessible[neighbor_pixel] = true;
           neighbor_level = imgData[neighbor_pixel];

           if (neighbor_level >= current_level)
           {
            boundary_pixel[neighbor_level].push_back(neighbor_pixel);
            boundary_edge[neighbor_level].push_back(0);

              if (neighbor_level < priority)
                 priority = neighbor_level;
           }
           else
           {
            boundary_pixel[current_level].push_back(current_pixel);
            boundary_edge[current_level].push_back(current_edge + 1);

              if (current_level < priority)
                 priority = current_level;
```

Chapter 5: 4 techniques to become a code speed-reader

```
 99                current_pixel = neighbor_pixel;
100                current_level = neighbor_level;
101                current_edge = 0;
102                goto step_3;
103              }
104           }
105        }
106
107        //!< 5. Accumulate the current pixel to the component at the
108        //!<    top of the stack (water saturates the current pixel).
109        er_accumulate(er_stack.back(), current_pixel, x, y);
110
111        //!< 6. Pop the heap of boundary pixels. If the heap is empty,
112        //!<    we are done. If the returned pixel is at the same
113        //!<    grey - level as the previous, go to 4
114        if (priority == highest_level)
115        {
116          delete[] pixel_accessible;
117          return er_stack.back();
118        }
119
120
121        int new_pixel = boundary_pixel[priority].back();
122        int new_edge = boundary_edge[priority].back();
123        int new_pixel_grey_level = imgData[new_pixel];
124
125        boundary_pixel[priority].pop_back();
126        boundary_edge[priority].pop_back();
127
128        while (boundary_pixel[priority].empty() && priority < highest\
129        _level)
130           priority++;
131
132        current_pixel =  new_pixel;
133        current_edge = new_edge;
134        x = current_pixel % width;
135        y = current_pixel / width;
136
```

```
137         if (new_pixel_grey_level != current_level)
138         {
139             //!< 7. The returned pixel is at a higher grey-level,
140             //!< so we must now process all components on the component
141             //!< stack until we reach the higher grey - level.
142             //!< This is done with the ProcessStack sub - routine,
143             //!< see below.Then go to 4.
144             current_level = new_pixel_grey_level;
145             process_stack(new_pixel_grey_level, er_stack);
146         }
147     }
148 }
```

Let's filter on its control flow by hiding the lines that do not contain the following keywords: `if`, `else`, `for`, `while`, `do`, `switch`, `case`, `try`, `catch`.

Some text editors are able to perform this type of operation. In Vim for example, you can execute the following command:

```
1  :g!/\(\<if\>\|\<else\>\|\<for\>\|\<while\>\|\<do\>\|\<switch\>\|
2  \<case\>\|\<try\>\|\<catch\>\)/d
```

Alternatively, you can use the online control flow filter tool available on Fluent C++[13] where you can just paste in your code to filter.

Here is what the result of filtering the above function looks like (after removing a few comments and trimming the lines of the `cases` that didn't fit on the length of the book page):

---

[13]https://www.fluentcpp.com/control-flow-filter/

Chapter 5: 4 techniques to become a code speed-reader

```
1   for (;;)
2     for (; current_edge < 4; current_edge++)
3       switch (current_edge)
4         case right :
5         case bottom :
6         case left :
7         case top :
8           if (!pixel_accessible[neighbor_pixel] && neighbor_pixel != \
9   current_pixel)
10          if (neighbor_level >= current_level)
11            if (neighbor_level < priority)
12          else
13            if (current_level < priority)
14        if (priority == highest_level)
15        while (boundary_pixel[priority].empty() && priority < highest\
16  _level)
17        if (new_pixel_grey_level != current_level)
```

The resulting code is much shorter. For a first analysis, reading those few lines in detail is quicker than reading the whole function.

The first line of this result is a loop with no stop condition in its declaration, and contains all the rest of the control flow of the function. This seems like a structuring piece of information that you'd like to know right away when analysing the function. By contrast, this `for` loop is located at line 45 in the original function, which means that by reading it line by line we would have to go through quite a bit of code before encountering this piece of information.

Then there is a `for` loop on 4 types of edges that appear in the switch statement that follows: right, bottom, left and top.

The code then checks if a pixel in that given direction is accessible and compares "levels" with "priorities". It does something specific to the `highest_level`. Finally it does something related to a "grey level".

Of course, this doesn't tell everything about the function and some concepts (such as "grey level") need to be clarified by a further reading of the function's code if we want to understand them, or maybe by knowing more about the domain of that piece of software.

But we now have a hypothesis on the function's overall structure: it seems to move around in a picture by hopping from adjacent pixel to adjacent pixel, comparing "levels" and "priorities" along the way.

This may be enough if all you're after is a general idea of the function. And if you do need to understand the function in greater detail, having an idea beforehand about where the function is going is a useful help.

4) Distinguishing the main action of the function

In a function, **not all lines contain the main action**, sometimes far from that. Some lines are merely secondary quests, like getting a value, logging a piece of information, or preparing a secondary character. You don't want to spend time on those details when inspecting the function. Instead, you want to jump to the main action first.

To locate the main action, you can quickly scan every line of the function, and determine if it looks like the main action, even if with a gut feeling. The point is to do this check fast. If it doesn't feel like the main action, don't spend time on it, even if you don't understand all it does. It will become clearer later.

An important thing to note for this technique is that it's okay to be wrong. The point is to scan code quickly rather than having a 100% accuracy when determining which lines contributes to the main action and which don't.

Indeed, achieving a 100% understanding of a long function the first time you encounter it is not always a good objective. Of course, each piece of code that you understand is valuable, but its understanding incurs a cost, because it requires time. And having a perfect understanding of every single line of every function you come across in a codebase requires a lot of time, if possible at all.

The good news is that you can figure out a large part of a function in relatively little time. This follows the Pareto principle[14], also known as the 80-20 rule, that states that in many events across various disciplines including computer science, 80% of the effects are the results of 20% of the causes.

The 80-20 rule here means that, out of the total time it would take you to understand a function to perfection, 20% of this time should already bring you an understanding of 80% of the function's code. Understanding the remaining

---

[14] https://en.wikipedia.org/wiki/Pareto_principle

20% of the function would then require the other 80% of the time. Those are not hard numbers, and some even call this the 90-10 rule.

In practice, those first quickly acquired 80% of understanding represent the main responsibility of a function, its main action, and the remaining 20% are some edge cases it has to deal with, or intermediary constructs that don't carry a lot of meaning.

If your goal is to get an idea of what a function is about, for example to understand its role in the context of an another function that calls it, 80% of understanding is often enough. It's okay to leave out some corner cases during a first exploration.

Some functions are worth investing the necessary time to understand them entirely. For example, they can be functions that have a bug in a corner case and that you need to fix, functions that you choose to refactor, or high level functions that show the structure of an important feature of the application.

But for a first exploration of a given function, consider trading off the understanding of every single detail against the efficiency you will gain by limiting your focus to the main action.

In practice, since most of the action is located in a small subset of a function's lines of code, if you're not sure about what a given line means at all, just move on to the next. Chances are it is not the main action, and you can always go back to it later if necessary.

To illustrate this technique, let's find the lines that are likely to hold some important action in the `processAlignments` function.

As a reminder, here was the code of the function:

```java
 1  public synchronized void processAlignments(String chr,
 2  List<Alignment> alignments) {
 3
 4    Genome genome = GenomeManager.getInstance().getCurrentGenome();
 5    chr = genome == null ? chr : genome.getCanonicalChrName(chr);
 6
 7    Map<Integer,InsertionMarker> insertionMap=insertionMaps.get(chr);
 8    if(insertionMap == null) {
 9      insertionMap =  Collections.synchronizedMap(new HashMap<>());
10      insertionMaps.put(chr, insertionMap);
11    }
12    List<Integer> positions = positionsMap.get(chr);
13    if(positions == null) {
14      positions = new ArrayList<>();
15      positionsMap.put(chr, positions);
16    }
17
18    int minLength = 0;
19    if (PreferencesManager.getPreferences().getAsBoolean(SAM_HIDE_S\
20  MALL_INDEL)) {
21      minLength = PreferencesManager.getPreferences().getAsInt(SAM_\
22  SMALL_INDEL_BP_THRESHOLD);
23    }
24
25    for (Alignment a : alignments) {
26      AlignmentBlock[] blocks = a.getInsertions();
27      if (blocks != null) {
28        for (AlignmentBlock block : blocks) {
29
30          if (block.getBases().length < minLength) continue;
31
32          Integer key = block.getStart();
```

```
33          InsertionMarker insertionMarker = insertionMap.get(key);
34          if (insertionMarker == null) {
35            insertionMarker = new InsertionMarker(
36                    block.getStart(), block.getLength());
37            insertionMap.put(key, insertionMarker);
38            positions.add(block.getStart());
39          } else {
40            insertionMarker.size =
41                Math.max(insertionMarker.size, block.getLength());
42          }
43        }
44      }
45    }
46
47
48    positions.addAll(insertionMap.keySet());
49    positions.sort((o1, o2) -> o1 - o2);
50  }
```

Let's analyse its body line by line to determine where the action is:

```
1   Genome genome = GenomeManager.getInstance().getCurrentGenome();
```

This is a good example of a line that does **not** contain the main action. Indeed, all this line does is create an intermediary object that seems to refer to an existing one.

```
1   chr = genome == null ? chr : genome.getCanonicalChrName(chr);
```

Since this this line looks like an adjustment of the input parameter chr, it's probably more about setting up chr for the rest of the function than the main action itself. So we can skip over that line of code too without spending more time understanding it.

114Chapter 5: 4 techniques to become a code speed-reader

```
1   Map<Integer,InsertionMarker> insertionMap=insertionMaps.get(chr);
```

This looks like an important step: we use the input parameter to obtain a new object. We will consider this line part of the main action of the function.

```
1     if(insertionMap == null) {
```

This looks like an error case: `insertionMap` was not found. Since we want to know what the function is about, let's not worry about how the function deals with special cases for the moment. We don't include them in the main action. We can therefore skip over the body of the if statement:

```
1       insertionMap = Collections.synchronizedMap(new HashMap<>());
2       insertionMaps.put(chr, insertionMap);
3     }
```

This leads us to the following line:

```
1     List<Integer> positions = positionsMap.get(chr);
```

Like the line that created `insertionMap`, this line looks important because it obtains an object based on the function's input. Let's consider it part of the main action.

```
1     if(positions == null) {
```

An error case again. Since we don't linger on special cases, we can skip this if statement:

```
1       positions = new ArrayList<>();
2       positionsMap.put(chr, positions);
3    }
```

This leads us to the following line:

```
1    int minLength = 0;
```

This is a simple initialization of a variable to 0. This is only set-up code, and not the main action of the function.

```
1       if (PreferencesManager.getPreferences().getAsBoolean(SAM_HIDE_S\
2    MALL_INDEL)) {
```

This line looks relatively complex because it involves unfamiliar terms such as SAM_HIDE_SMALL_INDEL. Not knowing what the application does, this is not easy to understand. Let's just skip this line for the moment. If this sort of term turns out to occur often, we can always come back to this lines of code. But the point is just to scan through the function now.

```
1       minLength = PreferencesManager.getPreferences().getAsInt(SAM_\
2    SMALL_INDEL_BP_THRESHOLD);
3    }
```

Another unfamiliar term, SAM_SMALL_INDEL_BP_THRESHOLD, is occuring. But this is just to assign a value to minLength. At this point we don't know if minLength is central to the function. Let's just keep in mind that we've encountered it and move on.

116Chapter 5: 4 techniques to become a code speed-reader

```
for (Alignment a : alignments) {
```

A for loop contains action, and this one concerns one of the inputs of the function, `alignments`. We can therefore assume that the body of that for-loop contains important actions.

```
AlignmentBlock[] blocks = a.getInsertions();
```

This line retrieves an object from one of the inputs of the function. This line per se does not perform any action but the objects it creates will probably be involved in the main action of the function.

```
if (blocks != null) {
```

Testing that the object is not a null reference is about an error case. We don't worry about those in this analysis, so we move on.

```
for (AlignmentBlock block : blocks) {
```

This inner loop iterates over an object that we deemed important earlier. We will consider it as part of the main action.

```
if (block.getBases().length < minLength) continue;
```

This code looks like it is dealing with a special case, as it skips an iteration of the for loop if some condition is met. Let's not linger on this special case. Note that it uses `minLength`, and so far `minLength` did not seem to be involved in any central action of the function. No need to go back to its definition to spend more time on it for the moment.

```
Integer key = block.getStart();
```

Even though `key` comes indirectly from an input of the function (`alignments`), it is quite a few indirections away from it now. Should we consider it a central piece of the function? In doubt, let's just move on and see what is next.

```
InsertionMarker insertionMarker = insertionMap.get(key);
```

This is another intermediary object. We start losing the big picture of the function. Let's just move on and see where this gets us.

```
if (insertionMarker == null) {
```

At first glance, this test may look like it is dealing with an error case of an object not found. But peeking ahead, we can see that there is more code when the object is not found (in the "then" clause) than when it is found (in the "else" clause). For this reason, let's take a look at both clauses of the if statement:

Chapter 5: 4 techniques to become a code speed-reader

```
1    insertionMarker = new InsertionMarker(
2        block.getStart(), block.getLength());
```

This line only constructs a local object. Let's not consider it the main action.

```
1    insertionMap.put(key, insertionMarker);
```

Now this is some important action: an entry is inserted into a map, and what's more that map was obtained from one of the inputs of the function. At this point, it could be instructive to look back at the 5 previous lines, because they turned out to be connected with an important action.

```
1    positions.add(block.getStart());
```

This is also some important action: new data is added to `positions`, which was obtained from one of the inputs too.

```
1    } else {
2        insertionMarker.size =
3            Math.max(insertionMarker.size, block.getLength());
4    }
```

This line modifies the data of a map we deemed important, so we can include it in the main action too.

```
1        }
2       }
3      }
4
5      positions.addAll(insertionMap.keySet());
```

Some action seems to be going on here too: data is added to an object that was already involved in the main action.

```
1      positions.sort((o1, o2) -> o1 - o2);
2    }
```

Finally some of the data is sorted. Even though this has an effect of the result, let's consider it a post-treatment rather than the main action of the function.

In the analysis we just carried out, most of the lines were not considered as containing main actions. If we remove them from the code, what we're left with is this:

```
1   public synchronized void processAlignments(String chr,
2   List<Alignment> alignments) {
3
4     Map<Integer, InsertionMarker> insertionMap = insertionMaps.get(\
5   chr);
6     List<Integer> positions = positionsMap.get(chr);
7
8     for (Alignment a : alignments) {
9       for (AlignmentBlock block : blocks) {
10        Integer key = block.getStart();
11        InsertionMarker insertionMarker = insertionMap.get(key);
12        if (insertionMarker == null) {
13          insertionMarker = new InsertionMarker(
14              block.getStart(), block.getLength());
15          insertionMap.put(key, insertionMarker);
```

```
16          positions.add(block.getStart());
17        } else {
18          insertionMarker.size =
19            Math.max(insertionMarker.size, block.getLength());
20        }
21      }
22    }
23
24    positions.addAll(insertionMap.keySet());
25  }
```

The above is more pseudo-code than actual compiling code because so many lines were slashed away, but it illustrates that the action of the function was reduced to a small subset of its lines. The rest was just setting up intermediary variables and dealing with special cases. In a first scanning of the function, it was not necessary to invest time on those lines to see the big picture.

This analysis suggests that the main action of the function is to use chr to obtain an insertionMap and a positionMap. It then loops over the alignments to extract info from their blocks (in particular their start and length), to populate both those maps.

This code is close to the result that we obtained with techniques 1) and 2):

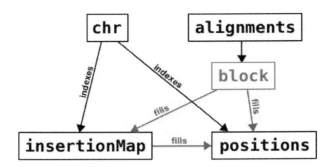

In some cases you may reach the end of the function without having found the main action because nothing looked like it. In this case, make a second pass with the same technique. Now that you have considered every line of the function and got a quick overview of its code, even if just a glance, the main action should stand out better than the first time.

Identifying the main action may be slow at the beginning. But the scanning of each line becomes much faster and more reliable with practice. With time, your eyes will scan over blocks of code rather than individual lines and you will be impressed at the speed you can scan code.

This is particularly true if you work on the same codebase for a period of time because you get used to its style. The coding style of the main action doesn't look like the coding style of the other bookkeeping stuff of the function.

Chapter 5: 4 techniques to become a code speed-reader

> **Key takeaways**
>
> - Start reading a function from its end.
> - Identify the terms that occur the most frequently in a piece of code, either by looking at the code or by using a tool.
> - Look for dense usages of the same term to understand the responsibilities of local chunks of code.
> - Reveal the structure of a piece of code by displaying only the lines that contain control flow keywords (`if`, `else`, `for`...) by using the a text editor or an specific tool.
> - Scan a piece of code by stopping only on lines that look like the "main action".

Chapter 6: 3 techniques to understand code in detail

The techniques we saw in Chapter 5 allow to quickly understand the general structure of a piece of code, and in many case that is all we need to do.

In some cases though, understanding the details of a piece of code is necessary. This is what this chapter is about, with the three following techniques:

- Using "practice" functions to improve your code-reading skills
- Decoupling the code
- Teaming up with other poeple

1) Using "practice" functions to improve your code-reading skills

What I call a "practice" function is a big function that has a complex implementation but that has little to no dependency on anything else. The function only goes so far and you don't have to get lost into another complex function and then another one and so on. It is self-contained.

Those functions are a great place to sharpen your skills of reading code. Even if their code looks cryptic at first, after some time you end up understanding and then mastering at least some parts of such a function.

This exercise of studying a practice room function has the effect of making you more familiar with the coding style of at least a part of the codebase, because it allows you to spend time studying in detail the same piece of code.

It doesn't mean that it is always a good model for writing your own code though, because some legacy codebases don't exactly have the best style. And you should also read good code independently from that, as we discussed in Chapter 3.

Studying "practice" functions will make your eyes get used to the patterns of the codebase, and you can benefit from this acquired familiarity when you explore other places in the codebase in order to read their code more quickly.

2) Decoupling the code

Refactoring is a great way to gain familiarity with a piece of code. But not all refactoring efforts will reward you with the same amount of knowledge for the time invested.

Indeed, while code cleanup has value, you will gain more useful knowledge from refactoring efforts that change the structure of the code (or sometimes it feels like putting a structure into place). One way to achieve this is by **decoupling** entities in the code.

You don't have to revise the architecture of the whole application to do this! There are several simpler ways to decouple components in code.

One possibility is to break down a function into sub-functions. This will give you a better overview of the sequencing of actions in this function, as well as a detailed view of the data that come into play in it. It can be useful for example to keep only the control flow in the original function and factor out each sub step or special case in its own separate well-named function. We will examine the reduction of long functions in detail in Chapter 13.

Another decoupling task that pays off a lot in terms of understanding code is to decouple data processing from objects. Let's now see this type of refactoring in detail.

A refactoring example

To illustrate the refactoring task of decoupling data processing from objects, we use an example of C++ code, inspired from production code but simplified in order to focus only on the part of the code we will refactor.

Consider the following `Order` class:

```cpp
class Order
{
public:
    Order(double price,
          Country const& originCountry,
          Country const& destinationCountry);

    double getTotalPrice() const;
    // ...
    void process();
    // other methods...

private:
    void processTaxes();

    // ...
    double price_;
    double totalPrice_;
    // ...
    Country originCountry_;
    Country destinationCountry_;
    // other attributes...
};
```

`Order` is a fairly big class, of which we only see a subset here. `Order` represents the purchase of a product between a buyer and a seller, and they may not be in the same country. An order has a price, an origin country (country of the seller) and a destination country (country of the buyer), amongst other attributes.

These attributes are initialized by the class constructor:

```
Order::Order(double price,
             Country const& originCountry,
             Country const& destinationCountry)
  : price_(price),
    originCountry_(originCountry),
    destinationCountry_(destinationCountry) {}
```

The Order class has a process method. In the middle of its code there is a call to another method, processTaxes:

```
void Order::process()
{
    // ...
    processTaxes();
    // other processing actions...
}
```

Finally, here is the body of processTaxes:

```cpp
1   void Order::processTaxes()
2   {
3     double taxValue
4       price_ * getTaxRate(destinationCountry_);
5     double internationalTaxCredit =
6       getInternatinalTaxCreditValue(price_,
7                                    originCountry_,
8                                    destinationCountry_);
9     double taxCut = getTaxCutRate(price_) * price_;
10    totalPrice_ = price_ + taxValue;
11    double taxReduction =
12      std::min(internationalTaxCredit + taxCut, taxValue);
13    totalPrice_ -= taxReduction;
14  }
```

The body of processTaxes performs various computations related to taxes, and it uses the attributes of Order extensively. You can see that because all the names ending with an underscore are attributes of Order.

In the code as it is, the computation of taxes has a high coupling with the Order class: processTaxes uses Order's attributes directly, and it would be hard to make another class use this code of taxes processing if necessary. We will therefore refactor the code to decouple the tax computation from the rest of the Order class.

As a first step to separate them, we can extract the processTaxes method out of the Order class.

```
 1  void processTaxes(Order& order)
 2  {
 3    double taxValue =
 4      order.getPrice() * getTaxRate(order.getDestinationCountry());
 5    double internationalTaxCredit =
 6      getInternatinalTaxCreditValue(order.getPrice(),
 7                                    order.getOriginCountry(),
 8                                    order.getDestinationCountry());
 9    double taxCut =
10      getTaxCutRate(order.getPrice()) * order.getPrice();
11    order.setTotalPrice(order.getPrice() + taxValue);
12    double taxReduction =
13      std::min(internationalTaxCredit + taxCut, taxValue);
14    order.setTotalPrice(order.getTotalPrice() - taxReduction);
15  }
```

In this first step of refactoring, we assume that Order has the necessary getters to access its members used by processTaxes, but we won't need them in the end anyway.

Even though it is no longer a private (nor a public) method of Order, this function remains coupled with Order because it accesses its data (via getters and setters). And another class than Order could still hardly use this code performing taxes computations.

Let's further reduce the coupling between processTaxes and the Order class. We will see how this refactoring task can help us better understand the code.

The idea to reduce coupling here is to make Order disappear from the code of processTaxes. To do this we examine what processTaxes uses in Order.

processTaxes uses four getters of order:

- `getPrice`
- `getOriginCountry`
- `getDestinationCountry`
- `getTotalPrice`

And one setter:

- `setTotalPrice`

This quick analysis suggests that the inputs of the function are the price, origin country, destination country, and total price of the order, and that the output of the function is to modify the total price of the order. At this stage, the difference of meaning between "price" and "total price" is not clear yet.

In the code as it is, the `order` plays the role of input and output of the function (it was also the case when it was a class method). Now that we have a clearer idea of the inputs and outputs of the tax computation, let's change the parameters of `processTaxes` so that it takes its input as parameters, and produce an output as return type.

The function prototype becomes:

```
double processTaxes(double price,
                    Country const& originCountry,
                    Country const& destinationCountry,
                    double totalPrice)
```

The function now returns the new total price. Its implementation becomes:

```
 1  double processTaxes(double price, Country const& originCountry,
 2      Country const& destinationCountry, double totalPrice)
 3  {
 4    double taxValue =
 5      price * getTaxRate(destinationCountry);
 6    double internationalTaxCredit =
 7      getInternatinalTaxCreditValue(price,
 8                                    originCountry,
 9                                    destinationCountry);
10    double taxCut = getTaxCutRate(price) * price;
11    totalPrice = price + taxValue;
12    double taxReduction =
13      std::min(internationalTaxCredit + taxCut, taxValue);
14    return totalPrice - taxReduction;
15  }
```

processTaxes no longer depends on Order.

We notice that the totalPrice parameter is never read before being overriden. It is therefore not an input, and we can remove it from the parameters of the function. The role of the function becomes clearer: it deduces a total price from a price and the information about countries, presumably by adding taxes to the price, based on the countries information.

With this insight and the new prototype, we can change processTaxes to a better name, for example priceAfter-Taxes, which is less vague.

```cpp
double priceAfterTaxes(double price, Country const& originCountry,
    Country const& destinationCountry)
{
  double taxValue =
    price * getTaxRate(destinationCountry);
  double internationalTaxCredit =
    getInternatinalTaxCreditValue(price,
                                  originCountry,
                                  destinationCountry);
  double taxCut = getTaxCutRate(price) * price;
  double totalPrice = price + taxValue;
  double taxReduction =
    std::min(internationalTaxCredit + taxCut, taxValue);
  return totalPrice - taxReduction;
}
```

As a final step of changing the code, we integrate this new function with the calling code in the process method of Order:

```cpp
void Order::process()
{
    // ...
    totalPrice_ = priceAfterTaxes(price_, originCountry_,
                                  destinationCountry_);
}
```

At this point we could also consider renaming total-Price_ into priceAfterTaxes_.

What refactoring this code taught us

Modifying the code the above way taught us several things about it.

First of all, it clarified the relation between `processTaxes` and `Order`, by exposing what the method was reading and modifying in the object. Knowing this is valuable, because this reduces the scope of action of `processTaxes`. Before the refactoring, it could theoretically interact with the whole `Order` class, a quite large class; after the refactoring, it can only interact with a handful of its attributes, which is easier to comprehend.

Another thing that this refactoring did is to remove the dependency that the code computing taxes had on the `Order` class. Indeed, now that we've changed the code, the computation of taxes no longer knows anything about the `Order` class. It is only the `Order` class that uses that code, and not the other way around. This is one less dependency to fit in our mental representation of the code, which makes is easier to understand.

We now get a better grasp of certain attributes, `price` and `totalPrice`, that had very similar names. We now know that `totalPrice` is equal to `prices` with taxes integrated. This piece of insight allowed us to clarify the role of the `processTaxes`, that had a vague name, and to give it a more precise one.

Reducing coupling has other benefits: it makes code simpler and more extensible. In the process, it provides insights on the details of the processing of a particular piece of data. It makes you learn a lot about the corresponding part of the program, both in terms of code and in terms of business features.

Note that this level of understanding is harder to attain by a simple reading of the code, without modifying it. The advantage of refactoring is that it makes you discover details when changing them, details that could be overlooked while reading through the code. Also, its incremental steps build on each other: going from one step to the other by updating code is easier than picturing the final code in one's mind all at once.

But refactoring code takes more time than reading it, especially since its requires testing to fix potential regressions after changing the code. And since you probably can't afford to refactor every piece of code that you need to understand, you need to decide where to invest your refactoring efforts. Chapter 12 presents some criteria to choose refactoring projects that bring the most value to your code.

For more refactoring ideas, *Refactoring* by Martin Fowler is a classical book on the subject. And since you need to have some tests to take on a refactoring project, refactoring legacy code goes hand in hand with the topic of tests, which you can read about in *Working effectively with legacy code* by Michael Feathers.

3) Teaming up with other people

After a while trying to figure out a piece of code on your own and not making sense of it, your incremental efforts to understand it may start to pay less. This is the law of diminishing returns.

At this point, it is beneficial to approach the code under a different angle. And what is more a different angle than the point of view of someone else?

Teaming up with another developer to understand a piece of code can be quite productive. It is not as widely spread as pair programming, but pairing for understanding code also has its certain advantages.

For one, you can capitalize on your previous efforts to understand the code on your own. Indeed, to get the person you have paired with up to speed, you will have to explain to them what you have understood so far. This will make you take a step back on the code and look at it with fresh eyes.

Sometimes this is enough to make you finally understand it. This is called the rubber-duck method[15] (because you could also explain your findings to a rubber duck), but a human being is often a better listener than a duck, as friendly as it may look.

If a mere explanation of your findings doesn't do it, working with the other person has several other advantages. One of them is that the other developer brings in their experience. Maybe they're familiar with this piece of code, or with that particular pattern. Or maybe they'll just see something that you did not, and you will complement each other and get to the end of it quickly.

---

[15] https://en.wikipedia.org/wiki/Rubber_duck_debugging

Indeed, teaming up for reading code is productive, because you do not get as easily distracted as when you're on your own. After a long time trying to decipher some code on your own, you may start to lose focus or get tired. On the other hand, when working with another developer, the constant interaction keeps you focused and productive.

It gets easier with practice

Even if tackling a large codebase that you haven't written yourself seems like a daunting task at first, it gets easier with time. The more code you master, the more you understand what the application is supposed to do, and the more easily you will assimilate new parts of it.

This needs time and a steady amount of effort. Find your stronghold, track inputs and outputs, analyse your stacks, read code like a non-fiction book, find the outputs of functions, identify the words that occur frequently, filter on control flow, focus on the main action, use "practice" functions to sharpen your skills, refactor the code by decoupling it to ease your understanding and team up with other developers. Then conquer the world map of your software.

Key takeaways

- Hone your skills of code analysis with "practice" functions, that is functions with complex code but no dependencies.
- Make a refactoring that decouples the code, to take a step back on the code and to get information on details.
- Team up with other poeple to put together experience and to stay focused and motivated.

Part III: Knowledge

Chapter 7: Knowledge is Power
Chapter 8: How to make knowledge flow in your team
Chapter 9: The Dailies: inject knowledge in regular doses

Chapter 7: Knowledge is Power

Scientia potentia est. This is Latin for "Knowledge is power", a quotation commonly attributed to Francis Bacon. But even if Mr Bacon never got to work with legacy code, his aphorism applies to it very well. When dealing with legacy code, knowledge of how existing code works is indeed power.

Let's return to our definition of legacy code to demonstrate this principle. We defined legacy code as code that:

1. is hard for you to understand,
2. you're not comfortable changing,
3. and you're somehow concerned with.

Why is legacy code hard to understand? Why are you not comfortable changing it?

The primary reason is lack of knowledge about how that code works.

This chapter demonstrates why knowledge is such a crucial factor in your ability to deal with legacy code, and the next two chapters will show you practical ways to grow your knowledge as well as the knowledge of every person in your team.

Being comfortable extracting knowledge from a legacy codebase will help you work in an effective and pleasant manner.

Where did the knowledge go?

The typical lack of knowledge associated with legacy code comes from several phenomena:

1. the knowledge handicap
2. the disappearance of knowledge
3. the uselessness of little knowledge
4. the vicious circle of losing knowledge

The Knowledge Handicap

When beginning a new job or starting to work on a new project, your specific-knowledge level resets to practically zero. And it's perfectly normal.

If a project starts at the same time as you begin working on it, then you're on par with the knowledge that exists about the project: you know nothing about how the code works, but there is also nothing to know about it because there is no code yet.

But this is not the most common case. Typically, you join a company or project that is already underway, and sometimes it has been for quite a long time. In that case, your knowledge no longer matches what there is to know, because the project has years of history behind it. In other words, we start projects with a knowledge handicap.

This is particularly true with legacy code, as legacy codebases tend to have years of history. Legacy code bases grew and evolved before you started to work on them. They can contain specific knowledge, approaches, and concepts that you haven't been exposed to on other projects.

But just because we start with a knowledge handicap doesn't mean we can't fill the gap! There are plenty of ways to get up to speed with the code, as we will see in the next chapters.

Knowledge goes away

It is important to be active in keeping knowledge around, and to spread it to every member of the team, because if we don't do anything about it, knowledge tends to fade away with time.

Indeed, if the codebase has been around for a long time, then there have been a lot of people working on it, potentially at different times. Each person was familiar with the pieces they worked on, but they might not be working on the project anymore. There are pieces of the code that were written by people that you can't talk to anymore.

Also, the knowledge possessed by a given person fades with time. If you have questions about a part of the codebase that looks mysterious to you, even if the person that worked on it is still around, they may not recall the context or rationale. But it makes sense: can you remember the details of the fixes you made 3 years ago? 7 years ago? 10 years ago?

If we don't do anything to prevent its loss, knowledge has a natural tendency to fade with time. This is why we need to be active in maintaining the level of knowledge of the team.

Little knowledge is next to no knowledge

Another reason why legacy code is hard to deal with is its complexity. Steve McConnell treats complexity as a central theme in *Code Complete*: software development is about managing complexity.

There are plenty of ways to manage complexity, such as encapsulation and levels of abstraction, but legacy codebases don't always have their complexity managed very well.

One aspect of this complexity is the **coupling** between the components of the code, whether implicit or explicit.

Explicit coupling is the coupling that shows in code: some piece of code has an intricate dependency on the functions and objects exposed by another part of the code. In this case you have to know all the coupled components as well as their interactions before you can call this knowledge useful. Indeed, knowing just one of the components is not enough to understand the big picture, nor to be comfortable changing it.

Even worse, coupling can also be implicit. This means that the dependency doesn't appear in code, but rather the internal behaviour of a component relies on the internal behaviour of another one. For example, it could be two functions that must be called in a particular order, even if their interfaces don't show any dependency on one another. This also requires you to know both components and their interaction, but since it didn't show, you may not know it until you broke something after changing one of the two coupled parts.

Either way, coupled components require you to know about *all* of them, as opposed to modular components that you can understand in isolation. With a complex coupled codebase, you need more knowledge to work with the code effectively.

There are several options to deal with this sort of situation. If a particular coupled piece of code qualifies as worthy of refactoring (see Chapter 12 about what to fix and what not to fix in legacy code) then you could change its design by decoupling it, and fix the problem. Even then, knowledge is a powerful resource.

But if this part of the code doesn't qualify for a refactoring, then your most practical tool is to *know* how the components work.

The lack of knowledge leads to chaos

As knowledge is power, conversely the lack of knowledge leads to chaos. And you don't want chaos to happen.

Chaos can look like this: lacking knowledge, a developer doesn't have control on their code. They feel unsure about how to change it and unexpected regressions get in their way. As a result, it takes a lot of time to perform a task that seemed simple at first. This causes developers to lose motivation. Past a certain point, some might leave and take away the bits of knowledge they managed to gather. This further reduces the amount of knowledge available to the team, which indirectly causes the code to become more complex: fewer and fewer developers understand the design intentions of the code, and the incremental changes may not follow the initial intentions. This creates inconsistencies, which slowly give chaos a firmer grasp on the codebase. As a result, the code becomes increasingly complex. And as we discussed above, complex (and coupled) systems are detrimental for maintaining knowledge.

You don't want such chaos to happen in your team. Instead, you want your team to be equipped with a healthy amount of knowledge. The good news is that there are ways to grow your knowledge. What's more, the more knowledge you have, the more you can accumulate.

Indeed, if you master the system, then everything is easier as you don't break the design when you change the code. You can then accumulate experience and grow your knowledge. And the fact that working with the code is easier can be a source of motivation for acquiring even more knowledge.

Knowledge is one of the most efficient tools to possess when working with legacy code. It is a precious resource, but if we don't do anything to maintain the knowledge level, it goes away.

In the next two chapters, we see how to maintain knowledge in your team, and how to make it grow, for you as well as every other member of your team.

Key takeaways

Lacking knowledge makes legacy code harder to work with. We lack knowledge because:

- We more often start on existing projects than on new projects.
- Knowledge gets lost as we forget things with time and people leave the company.
- Because of coupling, knowing one piece of code doesn't help if we don't know those it is coupled with.
- Due to the lack of knowledge, code modifications don't follow the intended design, creating even more things to know.

But there are ways to gain knowledge back.

Chapter 8: How to make knowledge flow in your team

Every line of code in the codebase has been written by someone. And each aspect of the design is the result of someone's reflection. So if you think about it, every last piece of knowledge about the codebase has been mastered by somebody, at some point.

Maybe some parts of the knowledge have become blurry, or are no longer available. But chances are some parts of that knowledge can be found somewhere around you. One person might not know everything, but if you sum up the knowledge that everyone in the team has ever owned, it can build up to a significant amount. If only there was a way for each member to acquire the sum of all this knowledge... it could really change things.

Unfortunately, human knowledge can't be as easily merged and copied around as sets do in software.

But there are ways to help getting closer to this ideal. This chapter presents efficient techniques to acquire knowledge: precious documentation, pair- and mob-programming, acquiring knowledge in Eager mode, acquiring knowledge in Lazy mode, and external sources.

Each of these is a deep topic, and we won't try to cover every last aspect here. Rather, we'll focus on how to use them to make knowledge flow around the team in an effective way.

The objective is to help you acquire knowledge in an easier way and, as a result, live a happier life as a software developer.

Writing precious documentation

Let's start with the topic of documentation. By documentation, here I mean documents outside of the code that describe how something works in the code.

It is generally seen to be a Good Thing to write documentation but at the same time, paradoxically, writing documentation is not the most popular activity amongst developers.

I think that to make sense of this curious paradox we have to adjust our perception of documentation. Writing documentation is not a Good Thing. Being nice to people is a Good Thing. Giving to charity is a Good Thing. And so is visiting your grandmother.

But there is no moral obligation to write documentation. We shouldn't do it because it's a Good Thing, as it's not. We should do it because it helps the business. Documentation helps you and the rest of the team be more efficient, and it even helps future teammates that will join the team one day.

What is important to realize is that not just any documentation is helpful. You want to create one specific type of documentation: **precious documentation**.

The opposite of precious documentation is useless documentation. Useless documentation suffers from several problems: it isn't read for various reasons (which we'll see below), it gets out of sync with the code, and it doesn't do you any good. In my opinion, useless documentation is what gives writing documentation such a bad reputation.

Fortunately, it is quite possible to write precious documentation, that is, documentation that gets read, doesn't get out of sync with the code too much, and benefits you. The following section explains how to combine those three aspects in your documentation.

Writing documentation that is read

To make sure that your documentation is effectively read, it needs to talk about something useful, not throw off the reader and to be found easily.

To achieve those three goals, let's see what topic to document, how to write in an appropriate style and where to put the documentation in a common location.

Chapter 8: How to make knowledge flow in your team

What topic to document

Let's start with what topic to write about. There are probably more topics about the code or the application than you could write about, even if you were spending 100% of your time writing documentation. You need to be selective about the the topics you choose to document.

One thing that is often useful to document is something that you had yourself trouble understanding, and that someone else has a chance to come across later. The more likely someone else will come across the same issue, the more useful the documentation.

This is also valid if that someone is yourself. If you've had to get really focused to understand how something complex was working, do you think you'll remember enough in a week to not have to analyze it again? What about in three years? Your busy future self will be grateful to read the compassionate writing of your past self that will spare him some tedious work.

Another source of inspiration for choosing a useful topic to write documentation about is getting the opinion of experienced people. Someone who knows their way around the codebase better should be able to tell what aspects of the design are fundamental: what you have to know, hat bits you need to understand so that things start clicking into place. You want to document that.

Writing style matters

The worst types of documentation I have read are those that feel like homework, made by someone who's been forced into writing documentation by their manager.

Going back to the moral obligation of writing documentation (or rather, the absence thereof), don't write a piece of documentation just because you have to, like at school, where you'd hand in an average paper for a course that you weren't too interested in.

Write the documentation that you wish you had read. If you see it as homework, aim for the highest grade. Use headers to make the structure of your write-up clearer. Write simple sentences. The goal is to be understood by someone who doesn't know what you're talking about. Indeed, this is your audience when you're writing documentation, because the people that are already familiar with the topic you're covering don't need to read documentation in the first place.

When you've finished your documentation, proofread it. If a sentence is not clear, it's useless, so make sure that everything is formulated as simply as possible. You're not expected to write like J. R. R. Tolkien, but if your writing is not clear enough, your readers will simply give up reading it.

If your documentation refers to code, make sure to have the functions and class names right. Don't make up new names because they look simpler, or else update the code with the new names first.

Indeed, a preliminary step of renaming in the code before writing documentation can be valuable. Once you have found a better name for an object in code, renaming is amongst the simplest refactoring tasks, so it doesn't cost a lot (see Chapter 12 on costs and values of refactoring projects). And renaming unclear names will spare the need to your documentation to clarify them.

When your documentation is all shiny and fresh from the oven, it's time to get feedback from other people, from your teammates from example. I recommend performing the same types of systematic reviews on documentation that you do for code reviews. You can often use the same tools.

A common location

Now that your documentation is about a useful topic and is written in a readable way, the last step is to make it reach its readers.

For this, the easiest solution is that all docs be at the same place, accessible to everyone. Indeed, if some docs are on a wiki, others in emails, and others in a local file on a developer's machine, they won't reach anyone and your efforts will have been for nothing.

The common place can be pretty much anything, but two possible options are the team's wiki, or in the same repository as the code itself.

The second option has the advantage of being modifiable alongside the code, in the same commit for example.

Writing documentation that doesn't get (too much) out of sync with the code

Another risk with documentation apart from the fact it's not read, is that it's read, but it tells a story that is different from the code.

If the code changes after you've written your documentation, and the documentation tells about something that doesn't exist anymore, the documentation is merely useless. But if it tells something that's the opposite of what the code is doing now, it becomes detrimental because it's misleading, and worse than no documentation at all.

So how to choose a topic that won't change too much in the near future? What if you don't have a crystal ball?

One way is to document a big picture view of the design. This tends to change more slowly than the nitty-gritty details of the code.

For instance, mentioning line numbers in your documentation is pretty pointless, because they change all the time.

Talking about a function's name is OK. It is useful while that function exists, even though its name may change at some point. But having an old version of the name is better than not having a name at all, because the old name still sits somewhere in the history of the code repository. If you talk about a function, make sure to add a little information about the context (a function called `save` or `readHeader` can be ambiguous if several functions share that name across the codebase).

Documenting how responsibilities are distributed amongst the various components of the program typically results in a document that is more dependable over time.

An empirical way to guess what should remain stable in a program is to check what hasn't changed in a while. If it hasn't changed for a long time, chances are that it's a pretty stable aspect of the code, and that it will remain close to what it is today for some time. This is called the Lindy Effect, where non-perishable things have a life expectancy proportional to their current age.

Writing documentation is cool

The perspective of writing documentation may seem daunting. But writing precious documentation is a nice thing, because it benefits you in many ways.

First, if you write a document about something that you know well in code, you will know it even better. Indeed, the process of transforming your collection of thoughts and bits of knowledge into a written structured document makes you to take a step back. You will likely encounter details that you weren't aware of, make connections to create a mental big picture, and even discover inconsistencies in the code that you hadn't seen at first glance.

But you don't have to be familiar with a topic to write documentation about it. You can examine an unknown part of the code that you need to become familiar with, and write documentation alongside your exploration. The action of documenting solidifies your findings, thus making the exploration go into a virtuous circle:

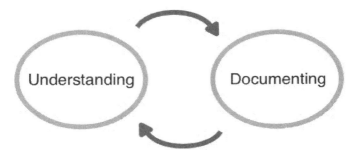

In such a case, writing documentation helps you expand your known territory inside of a legacy codebase. If there is a part of the code that you are not familiar with, you can see documenting it as a challenge. And at the end, you'll obtain a nice deliverable that will benefit everyone.

Writing documentation is also a nice way to gain visibility with other people, in particular if you are a younger developer. If you write a piece of documentation about a given topic, people will perceive you as knowledgeable on that topic. And if you take the initiative of writing a piece of documentation, your manager will likely be very pleased with you (this is my experience, both as a developer and a manager: managers tend to feel better when developers write documentation).

Now that we've talked about writing precious documentation, you need to make sure that it actually happens.

To this end, it is beneficial to put a process in place. Otherwise, other activities won't leave any bandwidth for documentation. Such a process can be as simple as fixing a rhythm of writing a piece of (hopefully) precious documentation every week.

That frequency can be applied for each developer, or to one developer of the team on a rotating scheme. This way, precious documentation will build up over time, and it will contribute to the amount of knowledge at the team's disposal.

Telling your tales: acquiring knowledge in Eager mode

Chances are that your total knowledge of your codebase contains some important information that your teammates don't have. Similarly, every member of your team has some knowledge or insight into your codebase that perhaps no one else knows either.

Why not tell each other what you know?

There is a lot to exchange, so you need some sort of framework to help knowledge flow around smoothly. For example, a weekly presentation from someone on the team contributes to a constant flow of precious knowledge in the team. This way, the amount of information builds up pretty quickly.

Note that the contents of such presentations can make a nice topic for writing documentation. You can also record those presentations in videos, which provides a great archive of resources for a new team member for example.

Knowing who to ask: getting knowledge in Lazy mode

When you need a piece of information, knowing who has it is a large part of the way to get the information you are looking for. Knowing which people are knowledgeable about each topic is extremely important, because it brings that knowledge within your reach with only a little investment.

It would be a shame if it turned out that the person sitting next to you knew the key to the problem you've been working on for days, and neither of you knows about what the other is working on.

One way to solve avoid this situation is to declare what topics you are knowledgeable about. There are several ways to go about that. An informal way is this: at each team meeting, go around the table so that each person shares what they're working on now. This way, you will regularly hear about the topics that your colleagues have at least some knowledge on.

The daily stand-up meeting from the Scrum methodology also allows, as a side effect, to know what everyone has been working on (even if its main goal is to decide what to do to meet the current sprint's objectives). If you'd like to read more about the Scrum methodology, you can refer to *Scrum: The Art of Doing Twice the Work in Half the Time* by Jeff Sutherland (co-creator of Scrum) and J. J. Sutherland.

Pair-programming and mob-programming

Pair-programming consists of two developers pairing up to solve a programming problem. They sit at the same computer and collaborate on the analysis and resolution of the problem at hand.

This practice has various implications on productivity, but what we'll focus on here is how pair-programming can allow passing knowledge around the team.

It is interesting to pair up with somebody that doesn't have the same skills as you. For example, it can be an experienced developer sitting with a junior developer, or two developers that are knowledgeable on different topics sitting together.

A collaboration such as this triggers questions from both sides, because each person observes the other one working in a different way than theirs. Those questions will be about the code, about techniques, about the application, and so on. The answers to those questions make the two developers learn, and grow their knowledge.

Pairing up with different people contributes to spread that knowledge amongst the team. If Alice pairs up with Bob and Bob learns something from Alice, then when Bob pairs up with Charlie the following time, Charlie can learn from Bob what he learnt from Alice.

You may not want to pair up for every task and might prefer to work alone from time to time, but a regular dose of pair-programming is healthy for the knowledge of the team.

An extension of pair-programming is mob-programming, which means more than two people working on the same programming problem on the same computer.

Even though they sound like similar activities, pair-programming and mob-programming really don't feel the same. Mob-programming feels more like a group tackling a problem as a team, as opposed to just people pairing up.

If you've never tried mob-programming, you should give it a go, at least once. Mob-programming offers many more angles to tackle problems. With the experience of the whole team put together, issues that would scare off a single developer seem a lot less daunting when combining everyone's knowledge. This lets you learn about the codebase, and lets everyone exchange their tips and tricks in a very natural way.

Note that when you do mob-programming, you need to be more organized because more people are participating. In particular, it's important to organize your time well. A convenient way is to make each developer have the keyboard in turn, with a timer to monitor when it's time to change. This allows a fair distribution of computer time.

In practice, we found that 7 minutes is a reasonable time for each turn: it is short enough so that everyone's turn comes quickly, and long enough to still have time to produce something when it is your turn.

External sources of knowledge

Some knowledge is specific to your codebase, but you can also benefit from knowledge that comes from the outside, and that happens to apply to your codebase too.

So where can you find information about how to tackle legacy code?

A good way to learn about this is to exchange with developers from outside of your company that also have to deal with legacy code. That means, pretty much every professional developer.

You can meet them at user groups and meetup. Visit the website meetup.com[16], and check out the meetups on software development around you. Some cities have a Software Craftsmanship meetup that is quite relevant for this. People

---
[16] https://www.meetup.com

in meetups are nice, and organizers go out of their way to make sure that you have a good time (as a meetup organizer, I can tell!).

Make the knowledge flow

Pick some of the above techniques to make knowledge circulate in your team. You will benefit from it, and so will your teammates.

Knowledge is power. Having it can make a difference in how you tackle a legacy codebase on an every day basis, and on how smoothly your life as a software developer goes.

May the Knowledge be with you!

Chapter 8: How to make knowledge flow in your team

Key takeaways

- Documentation is useful if it is read. For this choose a relevant topic, make it easy to read and find.
- To avoid that documentation gets out of sync with the code, document big picture views of the design or things that haven't changed for a while.
- Be aware of the beneficial side effects for you of writing documentation.
- Put a process in place (e.g. amount of produced documentation per week for the team).
- Organize regular informal presentations where a team member explains something he/she knows to the rest of the team
- Suggest that everyone declares what topics they're knowledgeable about, so that people know who to ask what.
- Do pair-programming and mob-programming sessions.
- Exchange with other developers at meetups and conferences, they also have legacy code.

Chapter 9: The Dailies: knowledge injected in regular doses

Developers are a pretty diversified species. There are web developers and software developers, developers in startups and developers in big companies, experienced veterans and fresh newbies, working on mobile apps, desktop apps, embedded components, operating systems... you name it.

Despite our diversity, there is one thing that we all share: we all love to learn things.

We read tons of books, blogs, and magazines; we watch hours and hours of videos, conferences, and live talks; we listen to podcasts every day, go to user groups several times a week, and have daily conversations with our co-workers or fellow students who are dripping with new insights on technology.

Sounds like your typical day? Most likely, you wish it did, but it doesn't. This probably sounds more like a dream schedule than day-to-day reality.

This is because there is something else we share as developers: we're busy. There is so much to do for work and

Chapter 9: The Dailies: knowledge injected in regular doses

sometimes it gets hard to dedicate as much time as we'd like to learning.

But the thing is, as a developer, if you don't learn regularly, you wilt - both in your skills and in your motivation.

Dailies allow to change the way we organize our learning in the workplace.

What are Dailies?

Dailies are live presentations made in the workplace that follow a set of rules. Those rules are designed to enable presenters to transfer knowledge to people who don't have much time.

Here are the rules:

- Dailies are presentations that last for about **10 minutes**.
- Dailies are given **every day**, once a day (hence the name).
- They are **internal** presentations, given by the people of the company to the people of the company. Most of the daily talks on a given topic are typically presented by the same person who takes charge of organizing, and they can have guest speakers.
- They are given **right in the office spaces**, where people actually work.
- They are packed into monthly sessions (more on this in a moment).

The topic of a Daily can be pretty much anything that can be split into small chunks: learning a language or a technology, explaining a big project you've worked on, and so on.

The main objective of these rules is making Dailies **easy to attend**. Short presentations allow the speaker to present information in little bites, the kind that can fit into a busy schedule. Pretty much everyone has 10 minutes available in their day. But these daily little pieces of knowledge build up over time, and after a couple of weeks, you will have learned a lot about a particular topic.

Moreover, the short format makes it easy to stay focused. The 10 minutes go by fast and people don't really have time to zone out.

And since a Daily occurs right in your office space, the only thing you have to do to attend it is turn back your chair, listen to the Daily for about 10 minutes, and then carry on with your day's work. Plus it creates a kind of cozy atmosphere:

Chapter 9: The Dailies: knowledge injected in regular doses

What can you do a Daily on? Pretty much anything: we've seen Dailies on Java, C++, Perl, functional programming, user interfaces, SQL, mathematical derivatives, Bitcoin, and so on.

What it takes to create a Daily is a team willing to spend 10 minutes listening to a presentation on a given topic every day in their office, and someone who is willing to present it to them every day over the course of a month.

Monthly sessions

Dailies are based on the principle that knowledge gets delivered to colleagues without them having to move every day to a training room.

So, to make their Daily available to every developer in a

company who is interested in a given topic, JavaScript for instance, the person who presents the Daily on JavaScript has to go from team to team to reach people.

To make this practical for everyone, Dailies are organized in **monthly sessions**. That is to say, the speaker gives all their presentations about JavaScript (for example) in October in their own office. The following month, they will visit another team's office every day, and deliver the **same content** to them. And so on, until they have gone to everyone who is interested in this topic.

To support these presentations, the speaker needs a set of 10 to 20 talks on their chosen subject, which they can deliver to the different teams. These talks can be filmed and uploaded somewhere so people are able to go back to them afterward, accompanied by a transcript, or the speaker can just present them if they don't have the time to develop supporting text or videos.

And when the speaker has gone to everyone, they can start over with a new set of 10 to 20 talks.

So in practice, at the beginning of a month, the speaker agrees with the team on a time (say, 11:00 a.m.) and schedules a meeting right there in the team's office space, every day, for the next 10 to 20 business days (depending on the size of the set of talks).

Then the speaker shows up on time and delivers their content for the day in about 10 minutes. Questions can be asked at the end of the Daily (except for the shorter ones), to respect everyone's time. In general, there won't be a projector in the team's office, so the best support to use during the presentation is a whiteboard.

The major benefits of Dailies

Those small chunks of information, delivered right to your office space, quickly build up over time and enrich your knowledge on a particular topic.

But Dailies also encourage communication: Since the speaker comes to your office, it's easy to go speak to them after the talks, ask your questions, and express your opinion on the topic of the day.

This is for attendees, but let's talk about how **presenting a Daily can be useful to you**.

One thing to remember is that you'll learn in the most efficient way by doing Dailies: by teaching. Presenting on a topic makes you assimilate it and gives you a deeper understanding of it.

Also, by hopping from team to team, you'll get to meet a lot of people along the way. I reckon I've met about 150 developers in my company who I wouldn't have known otherwise. And meeting all those people is a very enriching experience, for at least two reasons.

One, they share with you questions and remarks on the topic that you present, and this will give you new points of view on it. You'll get much deeper into your subject, and discover aspects you probably didn't know existed.

Two, those people who come up to you after your talk will be the ones who are passionate about the same topic as you. Meeting them will let you know who they are and give you some JavaScript friends (or Python, or C++, or whatever your topic is) in your company. And in such groups, you can learn a lot from each other.

By disseminating good coding practices through Dailies to all the people interested in acquiring this knowledge, you will make a real impact on the quality of the codebase of your company, because your fellow developers will be able to put the content of your talks into practice in their day-to-day work.

There is plenty of content out there

As you can imagine, even if 10 minutes is a short time, it can take time for the speaker to prepare, particularly if they're aiming to provide a transcript. For example, it takes me an average of two and a half hours to write a detailed transcript of a Daily session, like those you can find on Fluent C++ as indicated below.

But there is one type of existing content that typically fits into a 10-minute oral presentation and that can be found in abundance all over the internet: **blog posts**.

Blog posts are usually short pieces of information, and on specialized blogs you can find lots of articles going deep

Chapter 9: The Dailies: knowledge injected in regular doses

into a particular subject. Blogs are great learning resources.

But many developers don't read blogs on a regular basis. Dailies are a way to bring that content to the software developers who would benefit from it.

If you have the resources to produce your own content for Daily sessions, that's awesome. But if you don't have the time to produce 10 to 20 short talks every couple of months, then you can consider reusing the content on existing blogs.

As both a blogger and a Daily presenter, I use (amongst other blogs) the content on Fluent C++[17] to fuel the Daily C++ talks I give in my company. Feel free to use them, too. You'll find the most adapted posts flagged with this logo:

---

[17]https://www.fluentcpp.com/posts/

Be the one who spreads knowledge

Could you envision yourself animating a Daily session at your workplace and spreading bits of knowledge every day to the various teams of your company?

I've tried the experience and, frankly, it has changed my life as a software developer.

I have discovered a lot of things on C++ and on software development by preparing and presenting the sessions, and by meeting the people who attend my Daily sessions. I have met fantastic people with whom I now interact, and I see impacts on the codebase related to the topics we tackled in the presentations (for example more usages of C++ STL algorithms in the code).

Find relevant content or create your own, spread knowledge to your colleagues, become more well-versed on your subject matter, and meet passionate people. Be the one who motivates the spreading of knowledge in your team.

Chapter 9: The Dailies: knowledge injected in regular doses

Key takeaways

- Try Dailies in your company.
- Dailies are 10-minute presentations given every day to a team, for 10 to 20 days.
- The presentations occur right in the office spaces where people work.
- Go present the same contents to a new team every month.
- If you don't have the time to produce contents, reuse contents on blogs such as Fluent C++[a].

[a] https://www.fluentcpp.com/dailycpp

Part IV: Cutting through legacy code

Chapter 10: How to find the source of a bug without knowing a lot of code

Chapter 11: The Harmonica School: A case study in fixing a bug quickly in an unfamiliar code base

Chapter 12: What to fix and what *not* to fix in a legacy codebase

Chapter 13: 5 refactoring techniques to make long functions shorter

Chapter 10: How to find the source of a bug without knowing a lot of code

A lot of developers don't enjoy software maintenance. Maintenance is often associated with using the debugger to trudge through lines of code in a desperate search for bugs, usually in software that someone else wrote.

Maintenance has the reputation of being an unrewarding activity, with low intellectual stimulation. Many view it as less worthy of a developer's time than building a new feature.

I love maintenance. Not because I enjoy feeling lost in unfamiliar code, nor because I like spending hours running in circles.

I love maintenance because with the right techniques, it can be *fun*.

This chapter will show you an efficient maintenance technique. I initially learned it from software engineering literature (*Code Complete* by Steve McConnell in particular), and refined it by performing maintenance activities.

Chapter 10: How to find the source of a bug without knowing a lot of code

By improving the way we maintain software, you will come to enjoy fixing bugs in the application you're working on. I will show you how to save time and avoid frustration when working in maintenance mode.

The slowest way to find the source of a bug

Before we explore to the best approach to identifying the source of a bug, let's explore the natural approach. The natural approach goes like this:

1. You receive a bug report related feature X
2. You look around the code of feature X
3. You step through the codebase with the debugger, looking for the cause of the problem.

This approach is the least efficient way to find the cause of a bug. But this is our natural approach, and I have been guilty too of thrashing about with a debugger.

Why is this approach doomed to fail (or, at least to be a long and painful debugging adventure)? The simple reason is that **if you start by looking at the code, you don't know what you're looking for**. You hope to stumble upon the source of the problem by chance. You will probably find an unrelated problem that will make your debugging more confusing and send you on a wild goose chase. The most likely result is that you will get lost and not find any useful clues.

This approach to debugging is like looking for a specific street in a city, just by methodically walking around town until you run into that street. If you're in working a large legacy codebase, it's like walking in a big, big city. You may stumble upon the answer, but chances are you'll die of dehydration long before you find it.

The first piece of advice is therefore **don't start by looking at the code**. Instead, you want to begin by spending time analysing **the application while it is running**.

The quickest way to find the source of a bug

Now let's explore the process of debugging the application.

Step #1: Reproduce the issue

The first thing you want to look at in the application is **checking that the bug is there**. It sounds simple, but it happens that the development environment is not quite in the same configuration as the one where the bug appears. Any further analysis would be a waste of time, as you would be investigating with the wrong configuration.

Step #2: Perform differential testing to locate the issue

Once you've made sure that you do reproduce the bug, the next step is to **reduce the test case**. This consists in trying slight variations of the original test case in order to refine the scope of the bug. The goal is to identify the simplest test case which can reproduce the bug.

Step #2a: Start with a tiny difference

Let's see how to reduce a test case. We will illustrate this technique with a concrete example in Chapter 11.

Say that the bug is appearing in feature X when it is in config A1. Other possible configs of the feature X are A2, which is very close to A1, and B which is fairly different from A1. And A2 is simpler than A1.

Since A1 and A2 are so close, the bug will likely be reproduced with A2 too. But let's test A2 anyway.

If the bug is NOT reproduced in A2 then we know that the bug is specific to A1, and its cause lies in the difference between A1 and A2. If you can refine the test by checking another config A11 versus A12, then by all means do. Once you have checked all configurations, proceed to Step #3.

If the bug is also reproduced in A2, you know that the bug is not specific to A1 nor lies in the difference between A1 and A2. But you don't know where the source of the bug is yet, so we must continue to search for a reliable test case.

Step #2b: Continue with larger differences

Next we test larger configs, and **simpler ones if possible**. Consider Config B, for example. Since B is not close to A1, it's likely that you don't reproduce the bug in B.

But if you DO reproduce the bug in B, it means that the bug has nothing to do with A1. This is a common scenario when analysing bug reports.

This discovery brings you two new pieces of knowledge:

- it simplifies the test case in the event that we isolated the bug to config B
- it tells you that the bug is probably not related to feature X after all. We need to continue differential testing between feature X and another, close feature X2. And then a remote feature Y. And so on.

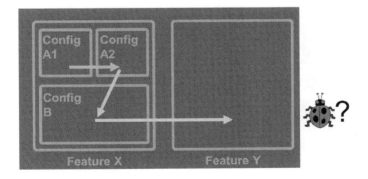

Step #3: Formulate and validate a hypothesis

Eventually we end up with a probable location for the bug and a method for reliably reproducing it. This is now the time to **formulate a hypothesis** about what is causing the incorrect behaviour. What could go wrong in this confined space of the application? If you see several things that go wrong, what's your gut feeling for which one is the most likely?

Only after this point in the process are you allowed to look at the code. The point of looking at the code is to confirm (or disprove) your hypothesis. Go directly to the portion of code that your differential testing pinpointed. Fire up the debugger and validate your hypothesis.

If your hypothesis was correct, congratulations, you identified the source of the bug! If it's not, repeat Step #3 until a hypothesis is successfully confirmed.

A binary search for the root cause of a bug

If you don't practice this technique or something resembling it yet, it probably sounds somewhat complicated. In that case, a nice analogy is to compare this with **linear search versus binary search**.

Starting by looking at the code and searching for what's

wrong in it is like **linear search**: you walk your way through the code, function by function or line by line, until you encounter the source of the issue.

However, with the method we described, that is operating with differential testing and hypotheses is like **binary search**: it consists in making checks at some targeted locations, and decide each time for a new direction to look into. And in the same way binary search eliminates huge chunks of the collection from the analysis, differential testing and hypotheses discard huge portions of the codebase that you won't have to look into.

This is what David Agans calls "Divide and Conquer" in its book *Debugging: The 9 Indispensable Rules for Finding Even the Most Elusive Software and Hardware Problems* : "[narrowing] the search by repeatedly splitting up the search space into a good half and a bad half, then looking further into the bad half for the problem."

Binary search takes more mental effort to implement than linear search. But a binary search strategy has two advantages: A) it's much faster and B) **it requires you to think**.

The latter advantage is what makes maintenance fun. Every bug becomes a sort of puzzle. But luckily it's a puzzle for which you have a method, and for which the resolution is only a matter of time.

A case study

Now that we've been through the successive steps of the method, let's see what it looks like when it's applied in practice.

For this, the next chapter goes through a concrete example of this bug-finding method to get some practice at applying it.

Key takeaways

- Exploring the code related to a buggy feature in search of the cause of the bug is inefficient.
- Start by verifying that you can reproduce the issue.
- Check if you still can reproduce the issue after a tiny change in configuration.
- If you still reproduce it, continue trying with bigger changes, until you no longer reproduce the issue.
- When you no longer reproduce, formulate a hypothesis about what is causing the problem.
- Only then look at the code, at the location to verify the hypothesis.

Chapter 11: The Harmonica School: A case study in diagnosing a bug quickly in an unfamiliar code base

The previous chapter described a method to find the source of a bug without looking at a lot of code. Here's a refresher of the method:

0) Don't start by looking at the code, start by looking at the running application

1. Reproduce the bug
2. Perform differential testing

2a) Start with a tiny difference
2b) Continue with larger differences

3. Formulate hypotheses and validate them in the code

Chapter 11: The Harmonica School: A case study in diagnosing a bug quickly in an unfamiliar code base

To help us contextualize this debugging method, we're going to work through a case study where we identify the root cause of a bug in a concrete example.

This case study is inspired by a bug that I found once while using an application. I've simplified the domain and the environment for presentation purposes, but the mechanics of the bug are the same.

The Harmonica School

Here's the story: you're a software developer working for the International School of Harmonica, which is a thriving establishment that delivers harmonica lessons to people around the world, that want to be able to master the subtleties of this musical instrument.

As a software developer for the International School of Harmonica, you have to maintain a large system that tracks what's going on in the school. And one day, you get a bug report. It's in the module that deals with lesson subscriptions.

Let's start by exploring how that feature works and reviewing the bug report. Next we'll apply our new debugging method to identify the source of the bug as quickly as possible.

Lesson subscriptions

When a student subscribes for harmonica lessons, the school inserts a subscription via a form in the system. The form looks like this:

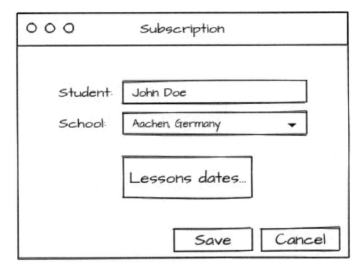

It contains the name of the student, the name of the school (which we'll identify with its city for simplicity here), and a button "Lessons dates..." that leads to the calendar of lessons that this student is subscribed to. Let's click on that "Lessons dates..." button. We see the following screen open:

Chapter 11: The Harmonica School: A case study in diagnosing a bug quickly in an unfamiliar code base

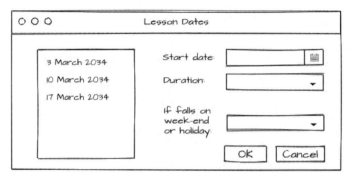

The left-hand side of this screen is taken up by the lesson schedule: these are the dates where the student is supposed to show up and learn how to express a myriad of emotions with their harmonica over an incredibly intense hour. For simplicity, we will leave out the lesson time in our example and focus only on the day.

The user can fill out the schedule manually, or they can use the right-hand side of the screen to generate dates automatically:

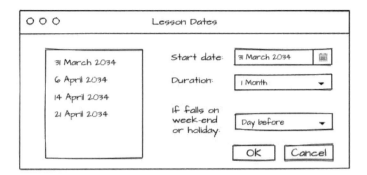

For simplicity's sake we assume that lessons occur on a weekly basis. Note that the 7th of April is Good Friday in Germany in 2034, but since the configuration of the right-hand side of the screen says that a lesson falling on a public holiday should be held the "day before" instead, the second date is the 6th of April.

That's it for the feature. Let's now have a look at that bug report.

The bug report

The bug report states:

> When we duplicate an existing lesson subscription and select another school for the A> newly created subscription, we observe that the lesson dates disappear.

> But we expect the duplicate to make a carbon copy of the subscription, which means A> also copying the dates.
>
> Note that if we only duplicate the subscription without changing the country, then the A> lesson dates remain.

Let's now apply our debugging method to find the source of that bug.

Let's find the source of that bug, quickly

Once more, a reminder of the method:

0) Don't start by looking at the code

1. Reproduce the bug
2. Perform differential testing

2a) Start with a tiny difference
2b) Continue with larger differences

3. Formulate hypotheses and validate them in the code

Step #0: Don't start by looking at the code

Let's go ahead and do 0) Don't start by looking at the code. That's the easiest one, since we don't do anything!

Now let's move on to 1) Reproduce the bug.

Step #1: Reproduce the bug

The test case contains a lesson subscription, let's see what's in it:

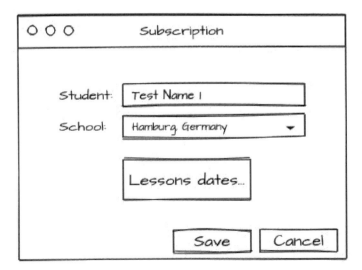

And the lessons dates look like this:

Chapter 11: The Harmonica School: A case study in diagnosing a bug quickly in an unfamiliar code base

```
┌─────────────────────────────────────────────┐
│ ○ ○ ○           Lesson Dates                │
├─────────────────────────────────────────────┤
│  ┌──────────────┐   Start date: ┌────────┐📅│
│  │ 1 April 2034 │                └────────┘  │
│  │ 6 April 2034 │   Duration:   ┌────────┐▼ │
│  │ 14 April 2034│                └────────┘  │
│  │              │   If falls on              │
│  │              │   week-end    ┌────────┐▼ │
│  │              │   or holiday: └────────┘  │
│  │              │           ┌────┐ ┌──────┐ │
│  └──────────────┘           │ OK │ │Cancel│ │
│                             └────┘ └──────┘ │
└─────────────────────────────────────────────┘
```

Those are entered manually and don't use the automatic generation.

Now we duplicate the subscription (say there is a UI action to perform that), give the duplicate a new name and change its country:

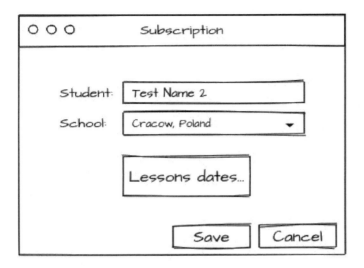

Let's now open the dates:

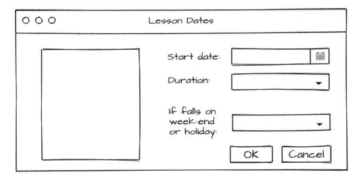

The dates are gone! Excellent, we can reproduce the issue. At this point, we can rejoice since the rest is only a matter of time.

Indeed, this is really a great position because things get harder when you **don't** reproduce the issue. When we don't find the bug, there are many more variables left to explore (configuration of your dev environment, wrong version in the version control system, misunderstanding of the test case, the test case can only be reproduced once in a given environment and you need to find a backup of the DB to restore... and other possibilities we can't even imagine).

But since we found a reproducible test case, we will hunt the bug down during step # 2: Perform differential testing.

Step #2: Perform differential testing

The bug report says that the issue happened when duplicating the lesson subscription. Is it specific to duplicates, or can it happen by simply inserting a subscription from scratch? The only way to know is to test it.

Let's insert a new subscription:

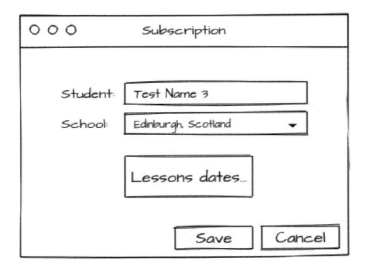

Let's fill out some dates:

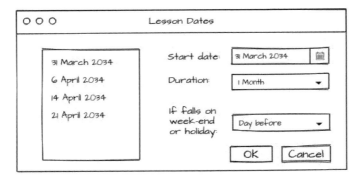

Now let's go back and change the country:

Chapter 11: The Harmonica School: A case study in diagnosing a bug quickly in an unfamiliar code base

```
┌─────────────────────────────────────────┐
│ ○ ○ ○          Subscription             │
├─────────────────────────────────────────┤
│                                         │
│      Student:  ┌──────────────┐         │
│                │ Test Name 3  │         │
│      School:   ├──────────────┴─┐       │
│                │ Paris, France ▼│       │
│                └────────────────┘       │
│                ┌──────────────┐         │
│                │Lessons dates…│         │
│                └──────────────┘         │
│                                         │
│                  ┌──────┐ ┌────────┐    │
│                  │ Save │ │ Cancel │    │
│                  └──────┘ └────────┘    │
└─────────────────────────────────────────┘
```

And reopen he dates:

```
┌─────────────────────────────────────────┐
│ ○ ○ ○          Lesson Dates             │
├─────────────────────────────────────────┤
│ ┌───────────┐   Start date: ┌───────┬─┐ │
│ │           │                └───────┴─┘│
│ │           │   Duration:   ┌─────────┐ │
│ │           │                └─────────┘│
│ │           │   If falls on              │
│ │           │   week-end    ┌─────────┐ │
│ │           │   or holiday:  └─────────┘│
│ └───────────┘      ┌────┐ ┌────────┐    │
│                    │ OK │ │ Cancel │    │
│                    └────┘ └────────┘    │
└─────────────────────────────────────────┘
```

Gone.

This indicates that the issue has nothing to do with the

duplication process. This is important because it represents a whole chunk of code we won't have to look at. Had we started with the code, we would have started debugging the duplication process. Now we know that it would have been a complete waste of time. This is why we always start by reproducing the bug, not by looking at code.

We can confirm our hypothesis even further by trying to change the country of an **existing** subscription. We won't get into the mock-ups for that test here, but it turns out that the bug is reproduced in this case too.

The bug happens when we change the country and open the dates screen. But are those two steps really necessary to reproduce the bug?

To check, we're going to perform each of them separately and see if we can reproduce the bug in each case. Let's start by changing the country without opening the dates.

To test this, we pick up the subscription from the test case:

Chapter 11: The Harmonica School: A case study in diagnosing a bug quickly in an unfamiliar code base

```
┌─────────────────────────────────────────────┐
│ O O O            Subscription               │
│                                             │
│       Student:  [ Test Name | ]             │
│       School:   [ Hamburg, Germany    ▼ ]   │
│                                             │
│                 [  Lessons dates...  ]      │
│                                             │
│                         [ Save ] [ Cancel ] │
└─────────────────────────────────────────────┘
```

We change its country:

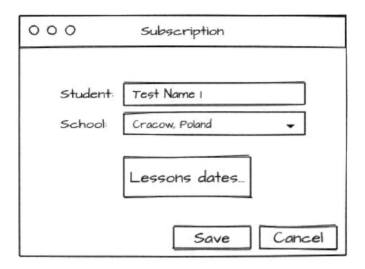

And we save it. Note that we didn't open the dates screen.

Now let's reopen the subscription and click to open the dates screen:

The dates are there, the bug is not reproduced, so it was necessary to open the dates screen right after changing the country. Opening the dates screen then flushes the dates.

But then, do we really need to change the country? Yes, because when we open a subscription and directly open the dates, we see that the dates are here, so the bug is not reproduced then. We saw that in the initial presentation of the feature.

We can deduce that opening the dates screen flushes the dates, but only if we've changed the country beforehand.

Now the question is: why? What's going on when we perform those two actions in a row? It's time to move on to step #3: Formulate hypotheses and validate them in the code.

Step #3: Formulate hypotheses and validate them in the code

Let's think: what is the link between a country and some dates? The first answer that comes to mind is public holidays. Indeed, each country has its public holidays.

To validate this hypothesis, we won't even have to look in the code. Looking in the code is typically slower than looking in the application, so let's save it for when there is nothing else we can do.

Different countries have different public holidays, but different **cities** in the same country may share some public holidays. Let's try to change the city without changing the country and see if we can reproduce the issue.

We start again with the subscription of the test case:

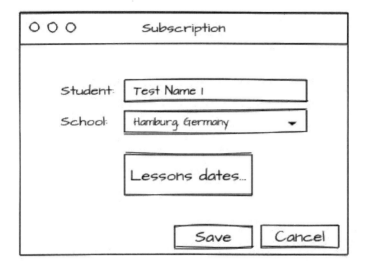

Note that we use the minimal test case that we obtained with differential testing. In particular, no need to go through duplication. We select another city in Germany:

Chapter 11: The Harmonica School: A case study in diagnosing a bug quickly in an unfamiliar code base

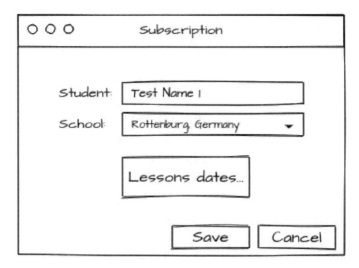

And open the dates screen:

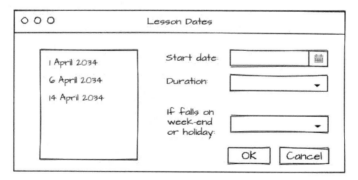

The dates are still there! The bug is not reproduced when we change city, only when we change country. This raises

the probability that the bug is somehow related to public holidays.

The other feature that is related to public holidays is the automatic generation of dates. Let's see if we can reproduce the issue with the generation parameters filled out.

We start again from the lesson subscription of the test case:

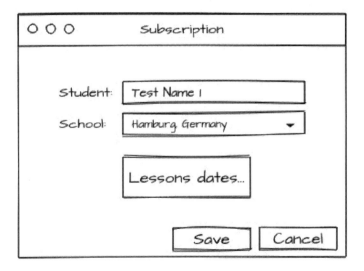

But this time we fill the generation parameters:

Chapter 11: The Harmonica School: A case study in diagnosing a bug quickly in an unfamiliar code base

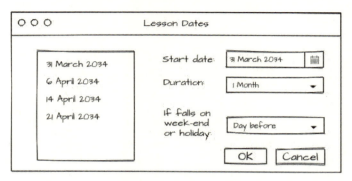

Now let's go back and change the country:

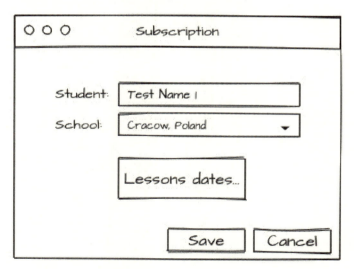

And reopen the dates screen:

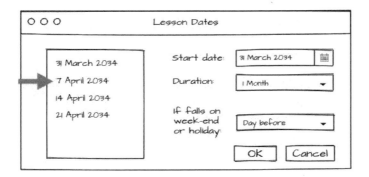

The dates are there, but not exactly the same. Unlike Germany, Poland doesn't have the 7th of April as a public holiday in 2034.

We can deduce that opening the dates screen is working out the dates based on the country and on the generation parameters.

Now we can formulate a hypothesis about the source of the bug: when we open the dates screen, the system tries to work out the generated dates if the country has changed. Something is going wrong when there are no generation parameters.

We can check this hypothesis in the code, and there is just a couple of lines that can confirm or refute the hypothesis. We go check that targeted portion of code, and it takes only a few minutes to realize that the system is trying to use an empty generator. The empty generator produces an empty set of dates, which the application happily accepts.

The source of the bug has been identified.

Chapter 11: The Harmonica School: A case study in diagnosing a bug quickly in an unfamiliar code base

Now we should think of a fix, but that's another story using another method.

The more time you spend in the application, the less total time you spend debugging

Even if I never worked for a school of harmonica, the bug I had seen in production looked essentially like this one, and all the above reasoning is very close to how the analysis went down. With this method, we could diagnose the bug in a matter of **minutes**.

When you do maintenance, don't start by looking at the code. Rather, play around with the application and reason about what test can help you narrow down the source of the issue. You'll save a lot of time and frustration in your life as a software developer.

Key takeaways

- Next time you have to diagnose a bug, don't start by searching for what's wrong in the code.
- Spend as much time as possible reducing the test case in the application.
- Only when you can no longer refine the test case, start looking at a targeted portion of code.

Chapter 12: What to fix and what *not* to fix in a legacy codebase

It makes me sad when I see competent and motivated developers losing faith and ending up suffering from the questionable quality of the code they're working on. Some resign themselves to despair and even spend years suffering from legacy code on a daily basis!

It doesn't have to be that way. One of the ways to get out of that spiral is not to let yourself be bullied by bad code.

Instead, show bad code who the boss is. This chapter will show you how to evaluate what refactoring projects are worthy of your time and can have the most positive impact on your codebase.

Chapter 12: What to fix and what *not* to fix in a legacy codebase

Legacy code is a bully

As a young developer starting to work in a codebase that has been there for a while (sometimes for longer than you've been alive) can be a challenge. Even more so when

you just graduated from CS school where you've mostly worked on libraries or ad-hoc projects. Being thrown all of a sudden into a big codebase that has evolved over years can be disorienting, to say the least.

It's like you're the new kid at school, and the big bullies don't plan on making your life easier.

Big functions, big objects, mysterious names, inconsistent and duplicate components, all those bullies stand in your way to your understanding of the code. They'll do all that is in their power to slow you down in your analysis; even when you make a fix and think you're done, they will throw an unexpected regression into your face.

But kids get bigger, bullies end up going out of school, and some kids even grow into the new bullies that will take care of the new generation.

This is where the metaphor breaks down. Even if you can grow as a developer, time doesn't make legacy code go anywhere. It's waiting for you, day in and day out, trying to get in your way.

If you're in that situation, I want you to take action by fixing the code. But not just any action. I want you to come up with a **targeted strategy**, that aims at making your legacy code less powerful in its ability to make your life difficult.

Let's see how to come up with that sort of strategy.

The value-based approach (a.k.a. "Hit it where it hurts")

There are so many things that you could fix in a legacy codebase. So many places would deserve a little makeover, or even a total refurbishing.

But there is a hard truth that you face one day:

You won't be able to fix it all.

It's not something that you realize at first. But there is a thing with codebases that took years of active work and involved several or many people: they're **vast**.

Fixing every last issue would take months, or years, and you have client requests to satisfy at the same time. Going off into a crusade trying to fix everything that's wrong in the codebase is a utopia.

Similarly, throwing it all to the bin and rewriting it from scratch is not always a realistic idea (as illustrated in details on Joel Spolsky's website amongst the Things You Should Never Do[18] Netscape did that, and... you don't really hear much about Netscape any more these days, do you?)

This is an idea that you need to settle in to. There is a high chance that some parts of your legacy codebase will sit there mostly untouched by anyone, for a long time. Like common "legacy" as in a piece of furniture that gets passed

---

[18] https://www.joelonsoftware.com/2000/04/06/things-you-should-never-do-part-i/

on from generation to generation. This is called legacy code, after all.

We won't debate whether this is good or bad. It's reality. Once you've accepted that you have to live with legacy code, you can take more rational decisions as to how to tackle that legacy codebase.

One practical consequence is that, however much time your company policy allows for refactoring, your resources are limited.

You're going to improve the code with refactoring, sure enough, but you need to make some choices about what pieces exactly you're going to use your bullets on. You need to pick your battles carefully, and reason about them. And evaluating which refactoring projects are worth your team's resources and which don't come down to a basic economic decision: **maximizing the value and minimizing the costs**.

Every refactoring brings value—hopefully—but also incurs a cost (which we'll see in a moment). The idea is to assess both the value and the cost, for each refactoring that you are considering. Once this is done, go for those that have the best value/cost ratios, and leave behind the refactorings that didn't make it through the economic decision.

Let's see how we evaluate the cost and the value of a refactoring project.

The costs of a refactoring

Let's start with the sources of costs of a refactoring project. That is, where it takes up some of your team's time.

There are some costs that we think about even before we start, like the time it takes to modify the code. But some other less obvious costs come up during execution, such as fixing regressions, adding tests and handling conflicts. We will analyse those sources of costs in detail.

Anticipating those costs will 1) lead you to choose optimal refactoring projects and 2) avoid the frustration coming from unexpected tasks that you're feeling are "getting in your way".

Those costs are typical of refactoring projects, but bear in mind that projects have "unknown unknowns". The following factors constitute a starting point for cost estimation rather than a comprehensive list for your next refactoring task.

The cost of understanding the existing code

If you're setting on a refactoring adventure, it means that the code you're putting your hands into is probably not the most explicit in the world.

And changing obscure code requires you to understand it first. If you're not clear about how that code works already, you need to take that analysis time into account.

How to analyse and understand legacy code is the subject of Chapters 4 to 6.

Fixing regressions

In our definition of legacy code (see introduction), legacy code is something you don't feel comfortable changing. And the reason why is that you suspect that changing it will cause regressions.

The cost of the regression depends on two things:

1. how long it takes to identify what caused the regression and
2. how long it takes to fix it.

Both those amounts of time are correlated with **how close your tests are to the code**. If the code you're changing has a lot of coverage by unit tests, it means you can get a fast feedback on your refactoring.

The sources of the regressions spotted by unit tests are fast to identify because unit tests can be launched often. Indeed, few changes happen between two successive launches, and therefore it's easy to spot where the regression comes from. And it's also fast to fix because you haven't had the time yet to build a lot upon the incorrect code.

The farther a test is from the code, the longer it takes to launch and the less often it's launched. Unit tests are launched more often than integration tests, which are themselves launched more often than system tests.

And the more time there is between two launches, the more happens in between. The specific fix causing the regression can then hide amongst many other fixes, becoming harder to identify. And you had time to build more code upon it, so fixing it has more impacts and takes longer.

The test that is the farthest from the code is when a client uses the software (well, this is not so much a test any more). Here, "client" is to be taken in the general sense as the user of your code. If you're developing a library, that would be your library user. Regressions discovered by a user are amongst the longest to identify and fix. To make things worse, they are also the ones that come in as interruptions and waste time by switching context with your other tasks, all that on top of hurting the public view of your product.

Adding tests

Speaking about tests, a refactoring that introduces boundaries and interfaces around a chunk of code may give you an opportunity to write some unit tests around it.

The time needed to write tests includes thinking of the scenarios to test and implementing them, but it's not only that. Most of the time taken in writing tests is doing that one last thing to cut off a dependency so that the code under test can be put into a test harness. And also that one last thing after it. And that last one after it. And so on. Chopping off dependencies can drag on and take a long time.

For a reference, Michael Feathers's *Working Effectively with Legacy Code* gives guidelines about how to cut dependencies in object-oriented languages (in particular for object oriented systems).

Handling conflicts

As we'll see below, good candidates for refactoring are regions of code that get in your way, one way or another. One example is regions of the codebase where you see a lot of bugs requests coming from users.

If you're doing your refactoring on that part of the code, there is a chance that someone else in the team may be fixing a bug at the same time not far from where you're working, since you're in a hot spot.

It doesn't mean that you should never refactor hot spots, quite the contrary. But it takes an effort of coordination. If everyone changes the same code in parallel, it becomes a nightmare to merge branches back into the master branch.

Some teams use the technique of a "development mutexes" to facilitate this coordination. It means that only one developer at a time is allowed to work on a refactoring on a hot spot. As a result, developers aren't allowed to exceed one or two days of lock time, which forces everyone to clean up the code in little packages only.

You can anticipate some conflicts to avoid them, but some conflicts are harder to anticipate than others, and you want to take this time into account in your estimate for the cost of refactoring.

The value of a refactoring

Now that we've gone over the costs of a refactoring, let's see what value we can get from a refactoring.

The point of a refactoring is to improve the quality of a region of the code. This brings up an important point: why do we strive for good code? Do we write good code for art, because it's beautiful? Do we write good code for morality, because it's wrong to write bad code?

No. **We should write good code because it helps the business.**

Good code leads to fewer bugs, faster integration of new features, less employee turnover in the company. All those things are beneficial to the business as in it generates financial benefits to your company and, in a lot of cases, to the users of your software as well.

A direct consequence of this is that **refactoring a piece of code that doesn't pose a problem (direct or indirect) to the business is a waste of time, energy, and money**. It's tantamount to refactoring the codebase of another company whilst we're at it.

The refactorings you want to choose are those that bring value to the business.

Paradoxically, the business doesn't know which refactoring will bring them value, because they don't know the state of the code as much as you do.

Actually, that's not entirely true. As we hinted earlier,

a region of code that corresponds to an unstable feature that has a lot of bugs is a great candidate for refactoring. Indeed, if you can make that code more structured and more expressive, you'll have more control over it, and hopefully fewer bugs.

Business people know *very well* what part of the application is causing them problems, and they'll be happy to tell you. This is important information that will allow you to identify valuable refactorings.

Other valuable refactorings are those that will let you do your job more efficiently. Of course, this means that you should select the refactoring tasks that will make your working with the code easier. But what this *also* means is that you should refrain from investing time in the refactoring projects that have a low value/cost ratio.

One example of refactoring is one that would diminish the capacity of the codebase to get in your way. We'll see more specific examples later, but it has to be code that you read – or debug – **frequently**. There is little point in refactoring code that you don't interact with often.

In particular, and it may sound surprising at first, **don't do a refactoring just because it is cheap**. If it doesn't bring enough value, you will have wasted time, energy and money.

It takes some will to steer away from the cheaper refactorings, because they are the most rewarding. You see how to make the code better, you feel it wouldn't be too hard, and you can almost feel the accomplishment of finishing this task and seeing the code changed.

If this sort of cheap refactoring also happens to bring a lot of value, then by all means, go ahead. But if there are other refactorings that would need more reflection but would make your life easier for your other developer tasks, resist the temptation and focus on the useful refactoring projects instead. We'll see in a moment some examples of refactoring tasks that tend to bring value.

You'll be more grateful to have spent an afternoon making one big hit to a targeted part of the code, rather than 50 little flicks all over the place.

Well, there is also another reason than the finances of business to improve code quality: good code makes our lives easier, as developers. Even if developers morale is also in the interest of the business, we can see it as a goal in itself for us programmers too.

In summary, you can't be only cost-driven (do the cheapest fixes) or only value-driven (only tackle the behemoths of the code). A good compromise is therefore to analyse **the value versus the cost of each refactoring**.

Start by picking the two or three things in your code that slow you down the most or are the most buggy, and that have a reasonable cost of refactoring.

One practical way to go about that is if every developer of the team marks off places in the code every time something related to the quality of the code slowed them down, while debugging or fixing a bug, or in any other development activity. Like by adding a cross in a comment whenever you stumble on code whose design is hindering you. A place with several crosses is a hot spot and likely slows many developers down. The hot spots show up this way.

Another way to identify hot spots is to look in your version control system what parts of the code tend to be modified very often, and to understand why they need more fixes than the rest of the code. If it is because they don't respect the Single Responsibility Principle or are otherwise poorly designed, they are relevant hot spots.

Other potential hot spots are those that come up in bug reports on a regular basis, as well as those where a lot of regressions appear.

Let's now see some typical examples of refactoring projects that could have a reasonable value/cost ratio.

Where does it hurt?

Before giving some suggestions, remember that you're the one in the best position to figure out your most valuable refactorings. What annoys you the most in your codebase on a daily basis?

Also, you can survey your team to ask their opinion on that question, and decide together on what to take action on. This has two benefits:

1. Team members feel involved in the strategy of refactoring, and
2. They are in the best position to say what is slowing down the team on a daily basis.

Here are some suggestions.

Slice up a big function

This is a classic one. Big functions drown readers of the code into low-level details and prevent them to have a big picture of what the function is doing.

Identifying the responsibilities of that function allows you to split it in several sub-functions and put explicit names on them, or outsource part of its work to another function or another object.

If you come across that function often, this refactoring can bring a lot of value. Refer to chapter 13 that shows 5 techniques to slice up a big function.

Slice up a big object

Some objects get extra responsibilities tacked on one by one over time, and evolve into massive behemoths that sit in the middle of the codebase.

Splitting their members allows you to manipulate lighter structures that take up less mental space in the mind of a reader.

Sometimes, slicing up a big function leads to slicing up a big object, if the various sub-functions operate on various, but distinct, parts of the object.

Make side effects visible

Big functions making side effects on big objects are notoriously hard to follow. Making it clear what effects a function has on objects helps following along and being less surprised when debugging code.

To do this you can use built-in features in languages, such as `const` in C++, to ensure that some objects cannot be modified.

Alternatively, you can pass in the objects to be modified as function argument instead of global variables. Or bundle the function that makes a side effect on a piece of data with it into a class. Or, if you can't do anything else, make it clear in a function's name what side effects it has (but that last method doesn't scale well).

Having no side effects is even better but, as a first step on a large function, this is not always a realistic target to aim for.

Use names that make sense

Poorly named objects can send you on a wrong track and make you waste a lot of time.

The value of changing some names can thus be high, and its cost varies from almost nothing for a local name, to higher if the codebase uses the name broadly and you don't have appropriate tooling to locate and change all the occurrences in one go.

Don't Repeat Yourself

Two (or more) identical pieces of code in the codebase means more code to become familiar with, more places for bugs to settle in, and more intellectual strain to fit everything in your head.

What's more, two or more pieces of duplicated code that start off as identical tend to evolve in separate directions. This makes code all the more difficult to manage.

You can make life easier by removing some duplicated logic across your module, or the codebase.

Removing duplicated logic can mean two things:

1. Merging two exact duplicates, that haven't had the time to diverge yet. This will prevent them for diverging, and make your future life easier.
2. Merging two non-identical duplicates, that have already diverged. This is harder to do because you need to find and extract what is common between them, or make them identical again somehow. But doing this relieves the codebase from obstacles to working with it.

In the attempt of mutualizing non-identical duplicates, a first step is to place them next to each other in code. Even if you stop there because going all the way would be too long, it is already a valuable move. Indeed, their being together makes it more likely that they won't diverge much more in the future, because other programmers will be at least aware of the existence of those duplicates.

If you'd like to see more refactoring patterns, you can find quite a lot of them in Martin Fowler's book *Refactoring*.

Get value now, pay the cost later

One team I know has an interesting technique to start reaping the value of a refactoring project even before they start touching the code. When they decide to introduce new abstractions in the code, but don't have the bandwidth to execute it now, they start talking about the code as if they had already put the new design in place.

This allows to share the vision of the target design among the team members early, and even with people outside of the team. The new abstractions are supposed to make the code easier to work with, and therefore also make technical discussions more productive.

What's more, articulating the new design allows the team members to refine it, and correct some aspects that looked good on paper. So when they do tackle the refactoring project, the design already have several weeks of maturity.

Use the value-based approach

In any case, don't let yourself be bullied by legacy or otherwise bad code. Use a rational approach, by identifying how you could change it by maximizing value and minimizing costs.

High value comes from the changes that help the business, directly or indirectly. Indirectly can be by allowing you as a developer to have an easier time working with the codebase.

Talk with your team, identify the painful points and how to fix them at a reasonable cost. Refrain from performing cheap refactoring tasks if you're not sure they're bringing tangible value. Start small, with a couple of bad functions or objects.

This way you'll get the most benefit from the efforts you invest in refactoring.

Key takeaways

- You can't refactor a whole legacy codebase, nor rewrite it all.
- You need a strategy to decide what to focus your refactoring efforts on.
- The useful refactorings are those that have a high value/cost ratio.
- Be aware of the various sources of cost of a refactoring task.
- A refactoring task brings value if it reduces the likelihood of bugs or if it makes your future tasks easier.
- Mark the places in code that make your life harder, they are candidates for refactoring.
- Don't refactor a piece of code just because it is easy to do so.
- Consider talking about the code in terms of the target design, even before you carry out a refactoring project.

Chapter 13: 5 refactoring techniques to make long functions shorter

One common pattern that makes legacy code hard to work with is long functions.

Many coding guidelines and experts recommend keeping functions short and focused on a single responsibility. The maximum recommended number of lines for a given function varies from company to company, and even from developer to developer, but they tend to be less than a couple of dozen of lines per function.

Functions in legacy code can reach far beyond any reasonable concept of "short". Some legacy codebases have some functions of hundreds, and even thousands of lines.

How are you supposed to understand a function that is 2000 lines long? By the time you've scrolled down to the end you've likely forgotten what was happening at the beginning. There are only so many details we can keep in mind at any given time.

Chapter 13: 5 refactoring techniques to make long functions shorter

In this chapter, you will learn how to reduce the size of long functions, in order to make them easier to work with.

The birth of a Behemoth

How could someone design a 2000 lines long function in the first place? The good news (and the bad news) is that they didn't: often, the functions slowly grow larger on their own.

What that means is that functions often start reasonably sized, well within the limit of lines recommended by whichever coding guidelines were in place at the time (if there were any). Over time software developers slowly make changes to the function, adding little bits here and there.

After the function reaches the clean code limit of size, the next developer who wants to add something is theoretically supposed reduce the size of the function.

But if their addition is small, like a single line of code, they may not recognize the need for restructuring the function to reduce its size. Or maybe there wasn't a clean code policy put in place. Whatever the reason, they don't refactor and the function grows out of the limit, if only a little.

As the function becomes bigger and bigger, at some point no one masters it entirely. From this point on, we don't even realize that it is getting bigger because it's already too large to have a mental representation of it. And it keeps growing.

This process is both good news and bad news. It's bad news because long functions tend to lack structure and organization, which make them difficult to understand. And you should as much as possible avoid allowing the rise of a Behemoth.

But it's also good news because most out-of-control functions ended up that way out of laziness. There likely are low-hanging fruit waiting to be picked: we can simplify long functions with reasonable effort. Let's explore techniques you can use to refactor long functions.

Identifying units of behaviour

Too much code in a function could mean either that the function has too many responsibilities, that it deals with too many details about its responsibilities, or perhaps a combination of the two.

If the function has too many responsibilities, to reduce its size we need to break up those responsibilities into two or more functions, and move the corresponding code. Remember that a good function has a single purpose.

But even when the function has a single responsibility, the code may still be too long because it has to deal with too many implementation details. Said differently, the level of abstraction of the function body is too low. In this case, a possible fix is to split apart this low level code to sub-functions (or objects), and make the function call these instead of dealing directly with the low level code.

Breaking up the code allows you to tidy up the code as well as shorten the function: each step of the function is implemented in its own unit, either as a free function or wrapped in a simple class, and that unit has a **name**. The initial function uses them to achieve its responsibilities and displays the names of the sub-functions and objects in its body, in order to show concisely what it achieves as a whole.

It is important to note that it is fine to move code into a sub-function even if this code is not duplicated and appears only once in the codebase. As C++ expert Tony van Eerd says, the minimum number of occurrences to justify putting a piece of code in its own function is 1. This practice also favours code reuse, as a newly formed function could be of use in other places in the code.

Moving code around may or may not reduce the size of the codebase as a whole. In some cases it will end up adding more lines by introducing new functions and objects for code that was not duplicated.

But the point of this chapter is not to reduce the size of the codebase as a whole (even if it would be a good thing). It is specifically about reducing the size of long functions, as that is what makes them hard to work with.

All the following refactorings have the same starting point: identifying the various **units of behaviour** of the function.

Once you have them identified, you can put them away in sub-functions or classes, and decide if it is the initial function that should call them, or another part of the code.

Let's see how to identify the various units of behaviour inside of a long function.

1) Extract `for` loops

By nature a `for` loop is a piece of code that holds some complexity. To understand it, you generally need to run it in your head, and human brains are nowhere as fast as CPUs to execute a `for` loop.

A `for` loop often represents a unit of behaviour in a long function, and taking it out into a separate function makes it easier to work with the code afterwards.

For this purpose, we can generally classify for loops into two categories: the loops that perform an algorithm (search, sort, etc.), and the loops that do a simple iteration on a collection and perform the same treatment to each element.

`for` loops representing algorithms

To get rid of a loop that performs an algorithm, use an existing implementation of this algorithm. Programming languages' standard libraries (such as C++'s STL) typically offer the common algorithms everyone uses on a daily basis.

Chapter 13: 5 refactoring techniques to make long functions shorter

There is generally no advantage in reimplementing standard algorithms, such as searching or sorting a collection, or any of the standard building blocks that all projects use.

For example, consider the following C++ code:

```
1   std::vector<int> numbers = {4, 2, 8, 15, 13, 3, 12};
2
3   int firstIndexGreaterThan10 = numbers.size();
4   for (size_t i = 0; i < numbers.size(); ++i)
5   {
6       if (numbers[i] > 10)
7       {
8           firstIndexGreaterThan10 = i;
9           break;
10      }
11  }
```

This code looks for the first index in the collection that corresponds to a value that is greater than 10, or the number of elements in the collection if no value greater than 10 is found.

Searching for the first position in a collection that satisfies a certain predicate is one of the most common tasks when manipulating collections. It is part of the C++ standard library, and using it allows to get rid of the `for` loop in our code:

```
1   auto firstElementGreaterThan10 = std::find_if(begin(numbers),
2       end(numbers), [](int number){return number > 10;});
3
4   auto firstIndexGreaterThan10 = std::distance(begin(numbers),
5       firstElementGreaterThan10);
```

For more elaborate examples of refactoring code to use standard algorithms, have a look at C++ expert Sean Parent's talk C++ Seasoning[19].

for **loops performing a simple iteration**

When considering for loops that don't perform an algorithm but simply iterate on a collection and apply the same treatment to each element, we can think of the loop as a unit of behaviour.

If the loop is complex and takes up a lot of space in the function, it could be worth moving it into a sub-function. Then if that sub-function has itself too many responsibilities we can recursively break it down too.

There is one case where taking the body of a for loop into a sub-function can be a problem: if the loop itself contains another for loop.

If a for loop contains a for loop, it may influence its algorithmic complexity (which is essentially the order of magnitude of the number of operations it performs). For instance, the fact that the code of a bubble sort has a

---

[19]https://channel9.msdn.com/Events/GoingNative/2013/Cpp-Seasoning

`for` loop that contains a `for` loop reflects its quadratic complexity.

This is something you may want to show in the code, and putting the body of the outer for loop in a separate function would hide this piece of information, and potentially lead to future changes in the code that would worsen the algorithmic complexity.

2) Extract intensive uses of the same object

As we saw in the chapters about understanding code, word counts reveal statistical information about your code. Their starting point consists in counting the number of occurrences of each term in a given piece of code, for example in a function.

For example consider the following class method taken from the igv open source project:

```java
public synchronized void processAlignments(String chr,
List<Alignment> alignments) {

    Genome genome = GenomeManager.getInstance().getCurrentGenome();
    chr = genome == null ? chr : genome.getCanonicalChrName(chr);

    Map<Integer,InsertionMarker> insertionMap=insertionMaps.get(chr);
    if(insertionMap == null) {
      insertionMap = Collections.synchronizedMap(new HashMap<>());
      insertionMaps.put(chr, insertionMap);
    }
    List<Integer> positions = positionsMap.get(chr);
    if(positions == null) {
      positions = new ArrayList<>();
      positionsMap.put(chr, positions);
    }

    int minLength = 0;
    if (PreferencesManager.getPreferences().getAsBoolean(SAM_HIDE_S\
MALL_INDEL)) {
       minLength = PreferencesManager.getPreferences().getAsInt(SAM_\
SMALL_INDEL_BP_THRESHOLD);
    }

    for (Alignment a : alignments) {
      AlignmentBlock[] blocks = a.getInsertions();
      if (blocks != null) {
        for (AlignmentBlock block : blocks) {

          if (block.getBases().length < minLength) continue;

          Integer key = block.getStart();
          InsertionMarker insertionMarker = insertionMap.get(key);
          if (insertionMarker == null) {
            insertionMarker = new InsertionMarker(
                    block.getStart(), block.getLength());
            insertionMap.put(key, insertionMarker);
            positions.add(block.getStart());
```

```
39            } else {
40                insertionMarker.size =
41                    Math.max(insertionMarker.size, block.getLength());
42            }
43        }
44    }
45  }
46
47
48    positions.addAll(insertionMap.keySet());
49    positions.sort((o1, o2) -> o1 - o2);
50 }
```

To perform a word count, we can either get an intuition of the frequent words by visually scanning the function or, if it is too long to be visually scanned, get hard numbers by performing an automatic word count. For long functions the second option gives more reliable (and faster) results.

To perform an automatic word count, we will use the word counter available on Fluent C++[20].

Here are the results of the automatic word count of the above function, for words that appear 3 times or more in its code:

---

[20]https://www.fluentcpp.com/word-count

Word	#
chr	8
insertionMap	7
block	7
positions	7
insertionMarker	6
if	6
null	5
key	3
InsertionMarker	3
Integer	3
minLength	3
put	3
get	3
genome	3
blocks	3
new	3
getStart	3

We now have the list of words that appear frequently in the function. To see if some specific regions of the function are using those terms, it would be also nice to know how spread out they are across the code of the function. For this we compute the span of each word, that is the number of lines over which it appears. For example, in the following piece of code:

```
1   int i = 42;
2   f(i);
3   f(i+1)
4   std::cout << "hello";
5   ++i;
```

The span of f is 2 because it first occurrence is at line 2 and its last one it at line 3. The span of i is 5 because its appearances start at line 1 and end at line 5. And the span of std::cout is 1 because it only appears on one line (line 4). In the general case, the span is equal to last line of appearance - first line of appearance + 1.

With the span we can compute the proportion that span takes in the length of the function. This proportion is the span divided by the total number of lines of the function, and can be expressed as a percentage.

Here are the results of our word count augmented with the span and proportion:

Word	#	span	proportion
chr	8	15	31.25%
insertionMap	7	40	83.33%
block	7	14	29.17%
positions	7	36	75%
insertionMarker	6	9	18.75%
if	6	25	52.08%
null	5	28	58.33%
key	3	6	12.5%
InsertionMarker	3	27	56.25%
Integer	3	24	50%
minLength	3	11	22.92%

Word	#	span	proportion
put	3	26	54.17%
get	3	25	52.08%
genome	3	2	4.17%
blocks	3	3	6.25%
new	3	25	52.08%
getStart	3	7	14.58%

The words with a high number of occurrences and low proportion are good leads for identifying some of the units of behaviour of the function. Since they appear often they probably play an important role, and since they don't occupy a large portion of the function their usage is rather intensive in that limited portion of the function.

Let's take the example of chr in the above code: it is the single most frequently occurring word (8 occurrences), and at the same time it has a relatively low proportion (31.25%) compared to the other frequent terms.

Here is the portion of code where chr appears:

```
1   Genome genome = GenomeManager.getInstance().getCurrentGenome();
2   chr = genome == null ? chr : genome.getCanonicalChrName(chr);
3
4   Map<Integer,InsertionMarker> insertionMap=insertionMaps.get(chr);
5   if(insertionMap == null) {
6       insertionMap = Collections.synchronizedMap(new HashMap<>());
7       insertionMaps.put(chr, insertionMap);
8   }
9   List<Integer> positions = positionsMap.get(chr);
10  if(positions == null) {
11      positions = new ArrayList<>();
12      positionsMap.put(chr, positions);
13  }
```

We see that `chr` plays an important role in this piece of code: it serves as an input to retrieve (or create) two collections.

This could be considered as a unit of behaviour in the class method, and could be taken out into a separate method. The role of this new method would be to take the `chr` and produce the two maps as outputs.

The second word that stands out has having a lot of occurrences and a low span and proportion is `block`. `block` is the iteration variable in the inner `for` loop of the second half of the function. This ties up well with technique 1) that suggested to look for `for` loops to identify units of behaviour.

3) Raise the level of abstraction in unbalanced `if` statements

In an `if` statement that has both an `if` branch and an `else` branch, we should expect the two branches to be at the same level of abstraction.

For example, consider the following code:

```
if (shouldUseDataBase)
{
    data = loadDataFromDataBase();
}
else
{
    data = loadDataFromFile();
}
```

The two branches of the if statement are at the same level of abstraction. They both express the loading of a piece of data. In contrast, consider this modified version of the same code:

```
if (useDataBase)
{
    bool isDataBaseOpened = openDataBaseConnection();
    if (isDataBaseOpened)
    {
        std::string sqlQuery = constructSqlQuery();
        data = loadDataFromDataBase(sqlQuery);
    }
    else
    {
        throw DBConnectionError();
    }
    closeDataBaseConnection();
}
else
{
    data = loadDataFromFile();
}
```

This code presumably achieves the same result as the first version, but it has a design issue: the two branches are not at the same level of abstraction.

To see this, consider the body of the if branch (the code that gets executed if the condition is true): it doesn't express *what* the algorithm does (loading from the database) but rather *how* it does it (opening the connection, building the SQL query, etc.). Whereas the else branch (the code that gets executed if the condition is false) expresses *what* it does (loading data from a file). The if branch is at a lower level of abstraction than the else branch.

An important principle of software engineering is to have consistent levels of abstraction, and this is why the first version of the code had a better design.

To raise the level of abstraction of the if branch of the second version, the fix consists in packing its code away in a function such as loadDataFromDataBase. This gives this piece of code a name that clearly states its purpose and hides the details of its implementation. The function's name should reflect *what* the code does and not *how* it does it.

To generalize this observation to other if statements, we should be on the lookout for if statements that have one branch that is much longer than the other branch. It could also be the else branch that gets into lower levels of abstraction. The visual pattern observed in the code is one of the two following shapes:

Unbalanced branch sizes don't always indicate a discrepancy in the levels of abstraction of the if statement. It could be that there *are* more things to do in either one of the two branches. And conversely, two branches of equivalent sizes could be of different levels of abstraction.

But since it takes more code to describe how to execute a task rather than what that task is, it is worth checking in the disproportionate if statement if the longer branch represents a unit of behaviour that could be packed away to reduce the size of the code it sits in.

Error cases

One notable exception to this rule is the case of very short branches that handle error cases. For example, consider the else statement in the following piece of code:

```
1   boolean isDataBaseOpened = openDataBaseConnection();
2   if (isDataBaseOpened)
3   {
4       String sqlQuery = constructSqlQuery();
5       data = loadDataFromDataBase(sqlQuery);
6   }
7   else
8   {
9       throw new RuntimeException("Cannot open database connection");
10  }
11  closeDataBaseConnection();
```

The fact that the else is short doesn't mean that its level of abstraction is inconsistent with the one of the if branch here. It is short because it is an error case, and all it does is trying to get out of the function as quickly as possible.

Still, those if statements are also good candidates for simplification: we can use guards (that is, short if statements at the beginning of the function) to separate the code of the error cases from the main code:

```
1   boolean isDataBaseOpened = openDataBaseConnection();
2   if (!isDataBaseOpened) throw new RuntimeException("Cannot open da\
3   tabase connection"); // <- this is the guard
4
5   String sqlQuery = constructSqlQuery();
6   data = loadDataFromDataBase(sqlQuery);
7   closeDataBaseConnection();
```

This way, all the error handling is dealt with before starting on the main action.

4) Lump up pieces of data that stick together

Some functions get very long because they contain repetitions of the same pattern over and over. Wrapping that pattern in a function or object, and using that wrapper each time instead of writing the whole pattern, allows us to cut down the length of the code by a large factor.

One example of such a pattern is when several pieces of data often get used together, such as the concepts of "value" and "currency" when representing money.

Let's take the example of a C++ function that has several usages of those piece of data. One usage is the assignment:

```
value2 = value1;
currency2 = currency1;
```

Another is the comparison:

```
assert(currency1 == currency2)
if (value1 == value2)
{
    ...
```

And another one is the sum:

```
assert(currency1 == currency2)
value3 = value1 + value2;
currency3 = currency1;
```

In this case, a value and a currency can be abstracted behind a concept: an amount of money. To reflect this in the code, we can introduce a class `Amount`:

```
class Amount
{
public:
    Amount(double value, std::string currency);
    double value() const;
    std::string const& currency() const;

    Amount& operator=(Amount const& other);
    bool operator==(Amount const& other);
    Amount operator+(Amount const& other);
    // ...

private:
    double value_;
    std::string currency_;
};
```

This class encapsulates the operations on the values and currencies that the initial function was performing. Here is the implementation of the methods of `Amount`:

```cpp
Amount::Amount(double value, std::string currency) :
    value_(value),
    currency_(std::move(currency))
    {}

double Amount::value() const
{
    return value_;
}

std::string const& Amount::currency() const
{
    return currency_;
}

Amount& Amount::operator=(Amount const& other)
{
    value_ = other.value_;
    currency_ = other.currency_;
    return *this;
}

bool Amount::operator==(Amount const& other)
{
    assert(currency_ == other.currency_);
    return value_ == other.value_;
}

Amount Amount::operator+(Amount const& other)
{
    assert(currency_ == other.currency_);
    return Amount(value_ + other.value_, currency_);
}
```

C++ offers the possibility to overload operators, which means that you can define the meaning of =, + or == for user-defined types such as amounts. For languages that don't allow this, you can still use classic member functions called `equal`, `add` and so on.

With the `Amount` class, we can replace the code using values and currencies in the initial function:

```
1   value2 = value1;
2   currency2 = currency1;
```

becomes

```
1   amount2 = amount1
```

Similarly,

```
1   assert(currency1 == currency2)
2   if (value1 == value2)
3   {
4       ...
```

becomes

```
1   if (amount1 == amount2)
2   {
3       ...
```

And

```
1    assert(currency1 == currency2)
2    value3 = value1 + value2;
3    currency3 = currency1;
```

becomes

```
1    amount3 = amount1 + amount2
```

This example uses only two pieces of data (`value` and `currency`). The more pieces of data encapsulated, the larger the cut on the length of the code.

Pieces of data that are always manipulated together in code don't necessarily correspond to one unified concept, but they are good candidates for deciding if they do. This removes the repetition of patterns and make the initial function code shorter.

Note that, with the above refactoring, the codebase hasn't reduced in size, and the code doesn't do less things. The logic was just moved from the original function to the `Amount` class, and this makes the initial function shorter and the system more understandable as a whole.

5) Follow the hints in the layout of the code

Some code shows its units of behaviour by relying on blank space to separate them from each other:

Chapter 13: 5 refactoring techniques to make long functions shorter

Each one of the "paragraphs" that compose this code could be a unit of behaviour, that could be put away in a separate function and called from here.

But a layout such as the one above one could also be incidental. A similar layout that is even more likely to show its units of behaviour is a set of spaced out blocks of code, each one being preceded by a comment:

Such comments that read "now we do this", "now we do that", helps identifying the role of each block of code. Often, they are an invitation to move their code to sub-functions and use the terms in the comments as a source of inspiration for naming those functions.

6) Bonus: using your IDE to hide code

I've seen people call this technique "cheating" because it is too easy. It allows to make long functions look short with no additional work, not by fixing them but by temporarily hiding the fact that they're long.

There is no rule of the game here. If a technique is useful to you then you should take advantage of it. Some developers find this technique useful, for example John Carmack who mentions it in his post on inlining (search for "editor collapsing" towards the end of his article). That said, if a piece of code forces you to hide its complexity to be able to read it, then you should also consider fixing it.

A lot of IDEs allow to collapse the code within a scope between braces ({}), typically with "-" buttons like this:

Those buttons allow to hide the code between brackets, allowing to see further down in the function without having to scroll down:

Some developers go as far as *adding braces* to the code that doesn't have (or need) any in order to apply this technique. They use those additional braces locally to collapse the code they surround in the IDE, but they don't commit those changes to the code repository.

Some editors allow to fold based on comments in the code. In Vim for example, the command `:set foldmethod=marker` makes the lines between commented triple braces (`/*{{{*/` and `/*}}}*/`) fold up.

Vim also allows to define what gets displayed instead of a folded portion of the code with the `foldtext` tag. For example you can display the first line of the folded code. Then if you write a comment on this first line, then this comment will be displayed instead of the folded block of code. For more details about how to execute this in Vim, type the command `:help fold-foldtext`.

This technique should be used with caution though. It might be part of the reason the behemoth is able to spawn and rise. If we abuse the technique of "just fold the code" it becomes easy to ignore those extra lines, or the for-loop-that-should-be-an-algorithm pattern for instance.

Also, fixing the code gives a more readable result than just collapsing it. For instance, if you take out a part of the function into a sub-function, then you see that call to the sub-function, with the name of the sub-function called in the initial function. The chunk of code is summarized into one line. As opposed to editor collapsing where you lose all the information about that part of the code.

The impact on performance

Most of the above suggestions for refactoring involve adding extra levels of indirection. After you performed those refactorings, to execute code that used to be part of the function the program now has to call sub-functions or class methods. This could in theory be detrimental for performance. Should this refrain you from performing the refactoring?

It depends, but in most cases the answer is No: you don't have to worry about this. But why? The application has to run fast enough, doesn't it?

It does. But in the majority of cases, the extra level of indirection doesn't make a difference. How so?

For some languages and with the right compiler options, the overhead coming from the call to a sub-function can be exactly equal to 0. This is the case in C++ for example, where compilers can inline the body of the function in some cases, which mean that they generate assembly code as if the moved code was still in the original function.

But even when there *is* a function call in the generated machine code, chances are its impact on performance is negligible. This is coming from the 80-20 rule in programming: 20% of the execution time is spent on 80% of the code. Some even go as far as considering this a 90-10 rule rather than 80-20.

This means that any given piece of code has more chances to be in a portion of the codebase that is not sensitive to performance rather than in a critical section. So in all likelihood, adding a level on indirection at a given place should be fine.

Moreover, breaking down long functions by outlining code allows to make profiling data more accurate to pinpoint the source of a performance bottleneck, making performance fixes easier to implement.

Even if they are rare, there *are* cases where adding an extra level of indirection has unacceptable impacts on performance. And the only way to identify them is by using a profiler.

If a profiler shows that the extra level of indirection you've added is detrimental for performance, you can always revert this particular change, and keep all the other changes that are beneficial to the code and neutral to performance.

Chapter 13: 5 refactoring techniques to make long functions shorter

Key takeaways

- Identify the units of behaviour that compose that function in order to take them out.
- Extract for loops to sub-functions, or replace them with calls to standard algorithms.
- Extract chunks of code that intensively use the same object, which you can identify with word counts with spans.
- If one of the two branches (the `if` or the `else`) of an if statement is much bigger than the other, consider extracting it.
- Create a class to put together pieces of data that are often used together.
- Extract blocks by following the hints in the layout of the code.
- Sacrifice code expressiveness only at the places where your profiling analysis tells you it is necessary.

Conclusion: The legacy of tomorrow

Let's do a little experiment. Think of a piece of legacy code from your code base, one that you find particularly hard to figure out and that you don't feel comfortable changing. It was written by someone, let's call that person Bill.

A long time ago, years ago, Bill wrote that little chunk of code that is giving you a hard time today. A long time ago, Bill wrote a piece of legacy code.

How do you think Bill was feeling the day he was writing it? Was he laughing diabolically, with lightning striking outside the window in the night, thunder rolling while he was typing away at his keyboard, thrilled at the idea of making your life harder several years down the line?

Probably not. Bill was a developer like you and me, writing code to solve a problem. And the code he wrote likely looked reasonable to him at the time.

Do you know the scariest part of this story? It's not the lightning, nor the thunder, and not even the unsettling laughter. The scary part is that if Bill was like you and me, it means that you and me are like Bill. And Bill wrote legacy code.

The bigger picture of writing code

The activity of writing code is not what it looks like at first.

At first, programming looks like it's about making a machine (computer, phone, car...) do something. We want a piece of software, we write code to make it, and it seems we're done with it.

But the activity of writing code doesn't stop there. It is even the opposite: taking control of a machine is only the beginning. And that's a skill that we acquire quite early on in our career as software developers. This is not the part that requires the most experience: the Internet is full of tutorials for learning any programming language, that any kid can take on.

But when we get past that first step, a new aspect in the activity of writing code kicks in: making code understandable by **humans** as well.

Making code manageable to humans is just as important as making it understandable to machines. Indeed, for a project to last, programmers need to collaborate on it in order to make it evolve. And even on a one-person project, the developer in charge needs to understand what his past self was doing.

So programming is about **communicating intents to humans**. And like in other types of communication, you need two things to get a message across from person A to person

B: person A needs to express it well, and person B needs to understand it well.

These two activities performed by person A and person B are the two fundamental aspects of the activity of writing code.

How to deal with legacy code

This book has been mostly focused on you being person B. Person B has a (legacy) codebase to figure out, and needs to take actions to create value while keeping a positive attitude.

We've seen the most efficient attitude for person B (Chapter 1), as well as how they can use bad code for their benefit (Chapter 3), although seeking out good code was also beneficial for inspiration (Chapter 4).

We went over 10 techniques to understand legacy code, in particular to get an overview of the code (Chapter 4), become a code speed-reader (Chapter 5) and understand code in detail (Chapter 6).

We've been over the power of knowledge for person B (Chapter 7) and how to harness it (Chapter 8 and 9).

And we've seen how to reduce the amount of code to understand while doing maintenance (Chapters 10 and 11), what parts of the code to fix to reduce the burden of understanding (Chapter 12) and how to make long functions shorter (Chapter 13).

But you're also person A

Every developer is both person A and person B: you write code and you read code. Sometimes you're playing the roles of both person A and person B for the same piece of code.

In your role as person A, you need to be able to express yourself in order to be understood as easily as possible. You need to write expressive code, and make good designs.

How to write expressive code?

This is a vast topic, and if you'd like to read more about it, have a look at Fluent C++[21].

Fluent C++ is a blog about writing expressive code. Even though it uses C++ to illustrate the techniques, a lot of its contents are applicable to any language. You can start by reading about levels of abstraction[22], or how to choose good names in code[23] for example.

Parting words

I hope this book will help you be more efficient, and happier, in your job as a software developer.

---

[21] https://www.fluentcpp.com
[22] https://www.fluentcpp.com/2016/12/15/respect-levels-of-abstraction/
[23] https://www.fluentcpp.com/2017/01/30/how-to-choose-good-names/

If you have a piece of feedback I'm very happy to hear it, you can send it to me via email at jonathan@fluentcpp.com[24].

Software development is a fascinating area, and the code written by other people at other times shouldn't hinder your passion for programming, quite the contrary. Adopt the right attitude, do what is in your power, and there is a lot, to do great things with your codebase, make successful software, and live on a happy developer life.

---

[24] mailto:jonathan@fluentcpp.com

References

Beautiful Code - Andy Oram, Greg Wilson (O'Reilly Media, 2007)

Clean Code - Robert C. Martin (Prentice Hall, 2008)

Code Complete - Steve McConnell (Microsoft Press, 2nd edition, 2004)

Debugging: The 9 Indispensable Rules for Finding Even the Most Elusive Software and Hardware Problems - David J. Agans (Amacom, 2006)

How to read a book - Mortimer J. Adler, Charles Van Doren (Touchstone, 1972)

John Carmack on Inlined Code (http://number-none.com/blow/john_carmack_on_inlined_code.html)

Scrum: The Art of Doing Twice the Work in Half the Time - Jeff Sutherland and J. J. Sutherland (Currency, 2014)

Refactoring - Martin Fowler (Addison-Wesley Professional, 1999)

The Art of Computer Programming - Donald E. Knuth (Addison-Wesley Professional, 2005)

Working Effectively with Legacy Code - Michael C. Feathers (Prentice Hall, 2004)

Made in the USA
Middletown, DE
24 February 2020

85238942R00165